BOOSTING MENTAL TOUGHNESS FOR TEENAGERS

REDUCE STRESS, TACKLE SOCIAL ANXIETY, CONQUER FEAR, AND BUILD SOCIAL CONFIDENCE

F. C. RAMIREZ

CONTENTS

Introduction   7

1. SELFIE LOVE   13
   Believe and Achieve   14
   Embrace Your Uniqueness   18
   Be Authentic   20
   Overcoming Negative Self-Talk   22

2. SELF-CARE 101   25
   Eat Well, Live Well   26
   Get Your Move On   29
   The Sleep Ninja   31

3. RISK IT TO WIN IT   35
   Embrace the Uncomfortable   37
   Learning From Failure   39
   Making Wise Decisions in Challenging Situations   41

4. BUSTING BULLIES   43
   Different Types of Bullying   45
   Behind the Mask   47
   From Victim to Survivor   49
   Online Warriors   51

5. SCHOOL SURVIVAL GUIDE   55
   Study Smarter, Not Harder   56
   Managing Exam Stress   58
   The Balancing Act   61

6. SUBSTANCE SMARTS   63
   From Pills to Puffs   64
   The Price of Substance Abuse   68
   Natural Highs   69
   Safe Havens   70

7. TRANSITIONS   73
The Beauty of Changing Your Environment   74
The Environment Shuffle   76
Friendship Remix   77

8. HORMONES, ZITS, AND GROWTH SPURTS   81
Shape-Shifting Shenanigans   82
A Storm of Emotions   84
Zit Happens   86
Funk-Free Revolution   87
TLC for the Teen Soul   88

9. DREAM IT, SEE IT, BE IT   91
Embracing the Bright Side   92
Create Your Dream Reality   95
Be Body Positive   97

10. BE THE BOSS OF YOUR BRAIN   99
What Is Emotional Intelligence?   100
Taming the Emotional Roller Coaster   103
The Anger Beast   105

11. STRESS BUSTERS   109
What Is Stress?   110
Zen Zone   110
Navigating the Shadows: Depression   114
Mindful Matters   115

12. FINDING YOUR TRIBE   119
Finding Your BFFs   120
Rise Above the Crowd   123
Settle Differences Like a Pro   125

13. FAMILY FEATS   131
Family Is Where It's At   132
Playing Your Part for a Harmonious Home   134
Redefining the Family: Thriving Without
Traditional Ties   136

14. SOCIAL MEDIA SAVVY   141
Cyber Citizenship   142
Unplug and Recharge   144

15. FUTURE FRONTIERS   147
    Discovering Your Passions: Exploring Career
    Options   148
    Mapping Your Path: SMART Goal Setting for
    Future Success   151
    Handling the Heat: Managing Pressure and
    Expectations   154

    Conclusion   159
    References   163

INTRODUCTION

Did you know that, as a teenager, you are a natural risk taker (Cleare, n.d.)? Your brain is wired to take risks! This teenage attribute has a scientific explanation. You are at a time when your brain is undergoing a major rewiring procedure that is meant to increase transmission speed while taking out connections that are unnecessary. When this rewiring process happens, the areas of the brain that are associated with decision-making and planning are attended to last. These regions, which are located in the frontal lobe of your brain, are in charge of your ability to make balanced decisions and weigh risks. The fact that this area is not fully functional in your brain is what makes you the natural risk-taker that you are. This probably explains why you need guidance from adults at this time of your life. However, while your risk-taking nature may make you vulnerable to different aspects that may negatively attack your physical, emotional, psychological, and spiritual well-being, you could turn it to your advantage. Mind you, risk-takers are survivors and are characterized by high self-esteem. There is a lot more that you can do!

Despite the fact that you have an attribute that could enhance your self-confidence, you might have a lot of self-doubt at the moment—not to worry, because that won't last long, especially after reading this book. Your currently low self-esteem may be because you constantly compare yourself with others regarding issues such as beauty, popularity, and intelligence, among others. Setting standards that are too high and striving for perfection may also contribute to self-doubt, especially when things don't go as expected.

Do you struggle with accepting setbacks, failure, and disappointments? If yes, you probably find it difficult to bounce back when things do not go according to plan. Persevering might also become an issue, as you take failures as a reflection of your personal inabilities. This not only contributes to self-blame but also creates a negative self-image in your mind. Many teenagers are also going through similar issues as you, so you are not all alone. The good news is that this book will assist you in seeing failures as part of the learning processes that make you better in life.

With the fast rate at which technology is moving, the internet has become a place where many teenagers spend much of their time, and you can possibly relate to this. With this in mind, cyberbullying has become prevalent, and you might have been a victim. Maybe not yet, but the fears associated with this form of bullying might be lurking around. Be it physical or cyberbullying, your emotional well-being becomes compromised. You might feel isolated, vulnerable, powerless, and humiliated, ultimately affecting your quality of life. This book will help you to regain your strength and navigate around issues to do with bullying. Remember, you are a risk taker!

Are you going through a lot of stress and anxiety? If yes, what you are feeling is nothing out of the ordinary, but it's important that you learn how to navigate through this dilemma. In the teenage years, stress and anxiety might be due to experiences that are associated with self-expectations, social interactions, academic pressure, and uncertainties about what the future holds. If you are looking for effective ways to reduce stress and anxiety and bring out the best in you, this book is the right tool for you.

Naturally, teenage years are associated with intense emotional development and hormonal changes. As a result, most teenagers struggle with emotional regulation, as they have to deal with various emotions, including anger, sadness, frustration, and disappointment. Does this describe what you are going through? This book will provide you with the tools that will help you to effectively cope with this emotional dilemma.

THE B.R.A.V.E.S.T. FRAMEWORK

This book presents a unique and effective way of dealing with any issues that threaten your well-being as a teenager. This comes in the form of what is called the B.R.A.V.E.S.T. framework. B.R.A.V.E.S.T. is an acronym that is defined as follows:

- **B:** Believe in yourself and feel good
- **R:** Resilience and grit
- **A:** Accept and adapt to change
- **V:** Visualization and positive thinking
- **E:** Emotional regulation and stress management
- **S:** Social matters and empathy
- **T:** Tomorrow and times to come

The B.R.A.V.E.S.T framework provides a comprehensive approach that addresses key aspects of personal development. This holistic approach recognizes that mental toughness encompasses multiple dimensions, including self-belief, emotional intelligence, cognitive flexibility, and interpersonal skills. By integrating these elements, the B.R.A.V.E.S.T framework offers you a well-rounded toolkit for developing mental toughness that goes beyond simplistic approaches, making it a unique and effective resource.

After applying the B.R.A.V.E.S.T framework to your life, there are various possible outcomes that you can expect. These include but are not limited to

- developing self-confidence and a deeper sense of belief in yourself.
- better adaptive thinking for creative problem solving and flexibility.
- developing a more positive mindset and visualization to drive motivation and goal attainment.
- improved emotional regulation and empathy for effective self-management and relationships.

- transformative personal growth and development.
- thriving in all aspects of life.
- overcoming obstacles with unwavering determination.

With this framework in your possession, there is nothing that can stop you from living your teenage life to the best of your ability. It's time to shine!

1

SELFIE LOVE

> *I haven't posted a selfie in a while but I still am very cute just to keep you updated.*

— ANONYMOUS

Although this might sound a bit like a brag, the bottom line of the statement is quite true. Posting a selfie might give self-esteem from external sources. When friends, relatives, and colleagues comment on how cute you look in your selfie, this might be enough to boost your self-confidence. However, this type of esteem cannot be relied on because it can disappear in an instant. For example, if people give you negative comments, even the little confidence that you had might vanish. When you still feel that you are cute, even without getting such endorsements from the external environment, then your self-esteem is classified as internal. Such confidence is more likely to stick around even in the midst of adversities. At least, no one can take what is within you.

In this chapter, we will address a part of the B.R.A.V.E.S.T framework, which is "Believe in yourself and feel good." To accomplish this, we will look at how you can develop a sense of self-appreciation and love. Some of the aspects that we will explore include embracing your uniqueness, being authentic, and overcoming negative self-talk.

BELIEVE AND ACHIEVE

Like any other human being, you have things that you can do. These things are your abilities. Now, believing in yourself simply refers to a state of mind where you have confidence in the set of abilities that you have. It involves trusting your ability to achieve desired outcomes. To be able to believe in yourself, you will certainly need to cultivate various attributes, which include autonomy, self-confidence, self-worth, self-respect, and environmental mastery. The first question in this regard would be, "How do I know whether I already have these attributes or not?" Well, here are a few questions that you can ask yourself to assess your

- **self-worth:** To what extent do I value myself as a human being?
- **self-confidence:** To what extent do I have my strength, skills, and abilities?
- **self-trust:** To what extent can I rely on my thoughts, beliefs, opinions, and actions?

- **autonomy:** To what extent do I feel independent and determined to undertake tasks and achieve my goals?
- **environmental mastery:** To what extent do I believe that my actions can result in desired outcomes?

As answers to these questions, select "strongly," "moderately," "poorly," or "not at all." As long as your answers fall into the last three categories, we recommend that you apply the tips that we will describe in this section to boost your belief in yourself and achieve your goals.

Practice Positive Self-Talk

Most self-talk is reflective of what you say about yourself. The more you learn to speak positively regarding yourself and your abilities, the greater the belief and trust that you develop toward yourself. You can use positive self-talk to oppose the negative inner voice in you. For example, if you feel that anyone else around you seems to carry out tasks better than you, audibly tell yourself, "I am able to do anything that I set my mind to." If you find yourself carried away by thoughts that are associated with an inferiority complex, remind yourself that you have what it takes to accomplish your goals and live your dreams. Mind you, some studies confirmed that positive self-talk tends to improve performance in any area of your life (Davis, 2022). Speak something positive to yourself each time you wake up.

Treat Yourself Kindly

Believing in yourself does not mean that you will never come across failures. You might, but you still need to remain kind to yourself after all. How you treat yourself in the face of adversity determines how you will bounce back. Furthermore, your ability to rise again after a fall does not only help you to believe in yourself more but it also increases your chances of living your life as an achiever, even during your adulthood.

Make Use of Your Positive Qualities and Strengths

Simply knowing that you have some strengths and good qualities is good enough to raise your self-belief to a higher level. Using your positive attributes practically is even better. Are you aware of your strengths? List all the strengths that you can remember. You can even ask a friend, colleague, sibling, or classmate that you can trust. They might know some of your strengths that you might not even know. Once you have the list, identify what you can do using your strengths and get to work. You don't need to apply all your strengths at once. One step at a time works better.

You might be tempted to think about your weaknesses, but don't dwell on that. Focusing on negative attributes will only escalate them. Likewise, concentrating on your positive characteristics is more likely to amplify them, too.

Honor Commitments and Be Honest

Think of how easy it is for you to trust people who appear to be honest with you. Imagine the amount of trust that you can possibly give to a person who always honors commitments. The same applies to you. Trusting yourself begins by being honest with regard to how you feel, what you think, and your actions. This will assist you to separate your likes and dislikes, in addition to identifying what you can do. If a friend invites you to a playdate, be there on time. If you do so consistently, the people around you will also notice as much as you do. This will grow the extent to which you believe in yourself.

Reclaim Your Power

Autonomy comes with the ability to govern yourself. The moment you think about governance, what comes into your mind? Power, right? In other words, there is no governance without power. This is why you need to reclaim the power that you might have lost to self-doubt. One of the effective ways of doing so is by associating with people who don't make you feel belittled and helpless. Surround yourself with people who help in bringing out the best in you. Sometimes, you simply have to believe against odds that are set by, say, culture. For instance, leadership positions tend to be predominantly taken by males. You might not believe you can take up the role of a leader in your class because you are female. Take up the post and challenge yourself. You will never know you can do something until you give it a shot!

Set Achievable Goals

Setting achievable goals assists you in gaining mastery over your environment. Remember, you want to train yourself to achieve results. If you set goals that are too high, you might become frustrated and gradually lose your self-belief. Start with smaller goals that you can achieve and then gradually aim higher as you go.

EMBRACE YOUR UNIQUENESS

Emily Delaney wrote an interesting short story that is titled "I'm a Short Afternoon Walk and You're Putting Way Too Much Pressure on Me" (Delaney, n.d.). In this story, the author describes how the afternoon walk usually starts as an adventure, a stress buster, or sometimes, an escape. As time goes on and people get used to the activity, they tend to expect too much from it. According to Delaney, they begin to expect it to be their "everything," which is more or less impossible. The author highlights that when people take their afternoon walks every afternoon, their emotions, thoughts, and intentions are never the same. As a result, each walk is, as expected, different from the previous one. However, expecting that all situations will be dealt with during the same afternoon walk can be a problem. Are you not treating yourself the same way people do to the "afternoon walk?" Are you not expecting yourself to be everything when, in actual fact, you can't be? In this section, we encourage you to embrace your uniqueness and be the best that you can be!

When you learn to embrace yourself for who you truly are, you are more likely to exhibit high levels of confidence. You can express yourself better when you learn to accept your individuality, and this usually leads to more positive outcomes. People who accept their uniqueness are among the happiest in the world. Let's explore how you can adopt the ability to embrace your uniqueness.

Discover What Makes You Special

Apparently, you can't embrace your uniqueness if you don't know what makes you special. The following questions can make it easy for you to come to terms with what separates you from others:

- What activities do you enjoy the most? Are there any reasons why these activities bring you joy?
- Is there something that you love about your appearance? What could that be and why?
- Who would you rather spend most of your time with?
- What talents do you have, and how can they be of help to people around you?
- Can you identify at least five strengths that you have and determine how they can help you achieve goals and live your dreams?

Accept Who You Are

Once you know what makes you unique, it's time to embrace it. Here are a few steps that you can follow:

- Accept yourself for who you are, and stop wishing you were someone else.
- As much as you can listen to the stories of others, remember that you have your unique one. Embrace that story.
- Stop trying to change yourself or compromise your beliefs to fit in certain situations, groups, and the like. You can't compromise your uniqueness.
- Surround yourself with people whose interests are similar to yours.
- Love and make the best of your skills and talents.
- Always prioritize doing what you love versus set obligations.
- Accept constructive criticism, and don't take it personally.

BE AUTHENTIC

Have you ever been to festivals where you have to wear a mask? Better still, if you have had a paint mask on before, then you have had a chance to hide from being yourself (at least artificially). So, being unauthentic is like making yourself and trying to be what you are not. On the other hand, being authentic requires you to be true to yourself. This takes being honest with yourself and others. Authentic people are not fond of the "blame game." They take full responsibility for the actions that they take. When you live authentically, you create room for genuine happiness, better mental health, and exploring your potential. You can easily earn respect and trust from others when you are authentic and boost your self-esteem.

It's important to know that living authentically is something that you develop over time. So, you don't need to beat yourself up if you feel that you are not authentic yet. Authenticity can be evaluated based on various aspects of your life, be it social, academic, careerwise, or even spiritual. You can determine your authenticity by asking yourself questions like these:

- What are the situations and activities that make me happy?
- Are there certain people who tend to light up the vibe in me?
- What are the things or situations that attract emotions such as sadness and anger?

Here is how you can start working toward being more authentic:

- **Uphold your values:** As a human being, you have your values, and being authentic involves respecting and living up to them. If staying out late doesn't make you feel comfortable, don't compromise.
- **Be vigilant when it comes to your goals:** Choose goals that align with your skills, abilities, and happiness. Avoid doing things just because everyone else seems to

do them. Ideally, choose goals that are specific, measurable, achievable, realistic, and time-related. Goals that have these five attributes are usually referred to as SMART, which is just an acronym for Specific, Measurable, Achievable, Relevant, and Timely (Hall, 2022).

- **Work on your emotional intelligence:** Emotional intelligence is one of the most important aspects of being authentic. Emotional intelligence involves being aware of your feelings and their triggers, as well as being mindful of others. Take some time to learn your emotional patterns, as well as how and when you need to control or express them.

- **Live your values:** You might have heard of the statement that says, "Do as I say, not as I do." Living by this statement shows a lack of authenticity. Rather, do what you say and value, be it at school, home, or work. This way, others will see the connection between your values and actions—that's authenticity!

OVERCOMING NEGATIVE SELF-TALK

Negative talk is quite detrimental to your self-esteem. Generally, negative talk comes in three forms, which are filtering, personalizing, and catastrophizing. Filtering involves only seeing the negative things, even if positivity is also evident. Personalizing involves the tendency to blame yourself for everything that does not go well. Catastrophizing is evident when your mind always imagines the worst-case scenario, even when it's not necessary. If you can identify with any of these types of negative talk, you can redeem yourself by applying the following tips:

- **Stalk your thought patterns:** Negative self-talk emanates from negative thought patterns. Therefore, to address negative self-talk from the roots, you should understand your thought patterns. This helps you to know the type of negative thoughts that usually overtake your mind. Once you are able to identify them, challenge them with positive self-affirmations each time they sneak into your mind again. For example, if you find yourself thinking badly about your physical appearance, you could tell yourself, "I am wonderfully and fearfully made. I am the best version."

- **Create a positive environment around yourself:** The people who stay around you are part of your environment. Surround yourself with people who can see the good in you. The more you are appreciated, the more you are likely to improve the way you think about yourself. This will end up reflecting in the words that you say.

- **Keep a record of your successes:** As much as you might think so bad about yourself, you do have accomplishments, don't you? Focus on your accolades and the things that you have done so well. Your accomplishments are great reminders of the fact that you can do it!

- **Engage in what boosts your mood:** What are the activities that make you happy? List them down and make time to engage in them more often. You are more likely to speak more positively about yourself when you are in a better mood.

It's time to give yourself some self-love! To do this, you need to learn to believe in yourself, be authentic, embrace your uniqueness, and do away with negative self-talk. Train yourself to think and speak well about your being, abilities, and goals. Having developed much love for who you are, you should take good care of yourself, and the next chapter will help you with that.

2

SELF-CARE 101

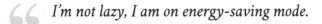 *I'm not lazy, I am on energy-saving mode.*

— ANONYMOUS

You probably chuckled at this. Well, being in an energy-saving mode is not bad, but hopefully, you are not forgetting to exercise, too. This is an important part of good self-care, as you will see in this chapter. Along with proper nutrition and quality sleep, regularly working out helps to maintain your physical, emotional, and psychological well-being. This chapter also contributes to the "B" part of the B.R.A.V.E.S.T. framework.

EAT WELL, LIVE WELL

Eating healthy has many benefits that you wouldn't want to miss out on. As a teenager, your body needs certain nutrients that enhance optimal growth and development. For example, you will still need calcium for strong bone formation. Mind you, you also need your brain to function well for better academic performance, among other things. Well, a well-balanced diet will help you achieve that. Good nutrition also helps to boost your energy levels. This is very important, especially if you are a sportsperson. Teenage years are associated with hormonal changes that require good nutrition for a good balance to be maintained.

You certainly want your body to be strong enough to ward off illnesses. There are foods that strengthen your immune system, giving it the leverage to fight infections. Some conditions, such as diabetes, can be avoided when you know what to eat and avoid. Acne breakouts are quite common during adolescence. However, you can save yourself from having to deal with it if you eat healthily.

Did you also know that your diet can affect your emotional patterns and mood? It is vital for you to eat foods that boost your mood and keep you emotionally stable. The best part is that you are learning to eat healthy at an early stage of your life, and you will reap the benefits, even in adulthood.

Highlights of Good Nutrition

You have probably heard about the fact that you should eat a healthy, balanced diet countless times now. In this section, we will try to be more specific with regard to the diet that is healthy for you as a teenager. This includes the type of nutrients that you should target as well as the portion sizes that are recommended.

- **Eat foods that are generally regarded as healthy:** Greens, especially vegetables and fruits, are an important part of your diet. The same applies to whole grains like barley, corn, oats, and unprocessed rice. These foods contain fiber, which aids good digestion, among other things. They also have antioxidants and vitamins that protect you from having to deal with heart diseases and some cancer later in life. As a teenager, you are still growing, so you will certainly need proteins. Good sources of proteins include beans, eggs, nuts, lean meat, chickpeas, and fish. You can even use vegetables, fruits, and nuts as your snacks, apart from including them in the main dishes.
- **Include calcium-rich foods:** To develop strong bones and teeth, you should consume foods that are rich in calcium and vitamin D. Milk, cheese, and yogurt are some such foods; no wonder why you should have five portions every day (Safefood, n.d.). Creative ways of including these foods in your diet include having a glass of milk during lunch or dinner. You could even add a slice of cheese to your favorite sandwiches!

- **Know the foods to limit:** Sugary drinks are quite attractive to many teenagers, but it's not good to consume them so often. Rather, go for fresh milk and water, as these two are much healthier. Did you know that the body of an average human being is made up of 60% water (Water Science School, 2019)? This means that limiting your water intake is detrimental to the normal functioning of your body. Fresh milk will also give you calcium and iron, both of which are good for bone development. Also, limit foods that contain added sugars, like cakes and ice cream. Too much added sugar increases your risk of contracting diseases like diabetes. You are also recommended to moderate your consumption of caffeine, especially through energy drinks. Research has shown that in every 500 milliliters of an energy drink, there are 17 teaspoons of sugar, in addition to two espresso cups worth of caffeine Moreover, a high intake of caffeine is associated with increased anxiety (Safefood, n.d.).
- **Include healthy fats:** Your body certainly needs fats, but you need to know which ones are healthy. Avocados, olive oil, and nuts are great sources of healthy fats. Avoid eating fats from margarine, bacon, poultry skin, and some deep-fried foods.
- **Include iron-rich foods:** The risk of low iron content is mainly an issue that affects teenage girls. However, all teenagers require iron because it is an energy booster that helps to support growth. Iron also aids in the excellent transportation of oxygen throughout the body. You can get plenty of iron from foods like eggs,

nuts, white meat, green vegetables, lentils, peas, and fish.

- **Embrace healthy eating habits:** Eating your breakfast every day is a good idea as it keeps you energized and focused unless you have to skip for certain reasons, which could be spiritual or otherwise. Also, be sure to monitor the sizes of the portions of food that you eat so that you keep your weight in check. Too large portions will see you getting obese.

GET YOUR MOVE ON

From just a walk to a jog, there are so many benefits of exercising. You can even make the endeavor more exciting by engaging in activities such as cycling and swimming to keep your body moving. If you are looking for exercise that requires less expensive equipment, rope skipping could be what you're looking for. You can even try various stretching exercises to flex your muscles and joints. Let's have a look at some of the benefits that are associated with exercising:

- **Healthy growth and development:** Exercise is good for your still-growing and developing body. For example, exercises such as dancing, jogging, and walking support the healthy development of your bones. Moreover, exercising is associated with greater brainpower (WebMD Editorial Contributors, 2023). You will also keep your muscles strong by exercising.
- **Healthy weight:** Working out enhances the rate at which your body uses up oxygen. As a result, your

body's metabolism also increases, creating a scenario that helps it to burn more calories within a given space of time. This is good for maintaining a healthy weight, which further protects you from the risk of diabetes, heart disease, stroke, and cataracts.

- **Boosting mental well-being:** When you exercise, your brain releases more endorphins, which are chemical substances that are known for improving mood. When endorphins are available in low concentrations, you become vulnerable to depression. Therefore, by exercising, you improve your mood while warding off depression and anxiety.

- **Improves cardiovascular health:** Cardiovascular exercises such as swimming, jogging, rope skipping, and cycling increase your heart and breathing rates. This trains the heart and lungs to be stronger, thereby making them more efficient.

- **Enhances cognitive function:** Exercising improves the rate at which nutrients and oxygen reach the brain. This also improves the efficiency of the brain waves that control your thinking. This means that the more you exercise, the quicker you are more likely to think. This way, your attention, focus, and academic performance also improve.

- **Boosts self-confidence:** You can engage in a good workout session as preparation for your presentation or any other task that requires higher levels of confidence. This is because exercising reduces negativity and increases your self-esteem.

- **Improved sleep patterns:** Research has shown that exercise improves the quality and quantity of sleep, both of which are of paramount importance. The quantity of sleep describes how long you can sleep, while the quality defines how deep you can rest (Johns Hopkins Medicine, n.d.). Engage in regular exercise and sleep better!
- **Enhances social interactions:** When you exercise in groups, you may end up developing sustainable connections that might help you in the future. The same applies when you engage in sporting activities where you will be part of a team. You will even learn to collaborate and work together with different people. That's an attribute that you will need for the rest of your life if you are to become successful.

THE SLEEP NINJA

You might laugh at the saying that goes like this: "If sleep is *so* important, why does school start so early" (Hudgins, 2021)? Interestingly, for you as a teenager, both school and sleep are vital. Therefore, since you cannot change the starting time for school, how about you go to sleep earlier so that you can benefit from both? There are many reasons why sleep is crucial for you. Most importantly, you need good sleep for healthy growth and development, as well as your overall well-being. Your brain function, learning abilities, and memory consolidation are at their best after quality sleep. Here are more benefits that are worth noting:

- **Boosting the immune system:** Your immune system is in a better position to fight attacks on your physical health when you sleep well.
- **Improving overall safety:** When you sleep well, you become more focused and alert. This improves your ability to drive and accomplish tasks without getting involved in accidents and other situations that put your life and health at risk.
- **Enhancing better emotional and mental health:** Lack of good sleep affects your mood, and this may cause irritability signs. Issues such as depression and anxiety might also appear. Therefore, getting enough sleep helps to curb these and many other issues.
- **Promoting better performance overall:** Considering that sleep improves focus, your academic performance is more likely to be positively impacted. Your overall take on life may also get better because problem-solving and decision-making acumen also improve.
- **Helping to regulate weight:** More sleep reduces the time that you will be roaming around looking for food. Resting through sleep also regulates the hormones that are associated with hunger and satiation (Pacheco, 2020). The hormone called leptin enhances appetite, while ghrelin triggers feelings of hunger. This regulation of sleep helps to control your weight.
- **Boosting energy:** After a good sleep, you are more likely to wake up feeling more energetic. This energy boost is quite good before sporting activities or any athletic performance. Sleep also promotes muscle growth.

Once upon a time, there was a woman whose teenage daughter, Candice, was struggling to lose weight. At some point, Candice's mother bought a small green basket and said to her daughter, "Each time you don't work out, place an apple in this basket." It was more like a little game, and Candice was happy to take part. By the end of the week, the basket was full of apples, and Candice showed the result to her mother, laughing. Her mother then said to her, "Each time you are eating much and avoiding exercise, this is how you are stuffing your body." This jolted Candice to a sudden realization that this could be the reason why she has been struggling to lose weight—uncontrolled eating and not honoring exercise schedules. Does your situation relate to Candice's?

Taking special care of yourself is a crucial aspect of boosting mental toughness. Basically, you should focus on eating and sleeping well, in addition to avoiding a completely sedentary lifestyle. Once you can take proper care of yourself, you then concentrate on building inner resilience, as discussed in the next chapter.

3

RISK IT TO WIN IT

> *Everything is funnier when you are not allowed to laugh.*
>
> — ANONYMOUS

As a teenager, it is only natural for you to take risks. You are going through new experiences, many of which require instant decisions. You have surely made some really bad decisions and choices along the way, and you will undoubtedly keep doing so as you approach adulthood. To live the life that you so desire, you will have to take many risks. However, there is a difference between calculated risks and irresponsible, foolish ones. Calculated risks require enough time to carefully think things through, while jumping toward something without giving prior regard to the consequences is not a wise thing to do. Please note that this chapter, in part, addresses "resilience and grit," which is the "R" part of the B.R.A.V.E.S.T. framework.

When you are convinced that something will work out, after carefully weighing all possibilities, it is time to take the risk and go for it. There will never be a perfect time when everything will be in place for you to start something new. You have to push for the changes yourself. The short story "The Forest and Her Children," by Dreyri Aldranaris, is a good example of just how taking a well-calculated risk can help you win in life. Azania was held in bondage and separated from her family against her will. Her masters saw her as nothing and constantly yelled at her, in addition to other forms of treating her badly. Despite this, Azania never showed any signs of disdain and still served her masters well. She pretended to be submissive and loyal while keeping all her disturbed emotions to herself.

Azania gradually gained her masters' trust until they were fully convinced of her loyalty. One day, she took all the money that was meant for buying items at the stores and made her way out of her masters' residence. No one suspected anything. There, she bought a wooden snorkel for breathing underwater and threw herself into the river. She disappeared for good. She had calculated her moves and carefully considered all the risks before pulling off a feat that no one ever expected. Nonetheless, she was free at long last. All the dreams that you have in mind are surely achievable. The biggest decision you need to make is committing to breaking away from your current comfortable situation at the earliest opportunity available.

EMBRACE THE UNCOMFORTABLE

You will only begin to truly grow in your academic, professional, and personal life the moment you decide to embrace new challenges. New challenges often come with lessons that will help you to develop into a better person. As a teenager, your body is slowly changing as you approach adulthood, with more hormones that trigger an increased need to try new things out. This is perfectly okay, and the only thing we encourage you to do is to carefully consider the risks before engaging in new adventures.

As you step outside of your comfort zone, the unfamiliarity you will encounter will improve your resilience to endure challenges, thereby making you stronger. Exposure to new things will also enhance your creativity, enabling you to discover new passions. As a young teen, most of your activities are usually prescribed for you. Thus, exploring new adventures is a good way to prescribe your own activities.

Create Your Trail

You can decide to move out of your comfort zone and embark on new activities of your choice to learn new skills. Once you do this, you will usually realize that you have other talents that you never knew of. These could form the foundation of your future career and lifestyle when you become an adult. New experiences in unfamiliar territory will challenge you in ways that will possibly push you toward many mistakes. Don't despair when that happens, as it is all part of learning. Setbacks and mistakes will actually teach you to do things better the next time.

Meeting new people will also help you to develop better communication skills and create new relationships. People from different backgrounds also have varied experiences that you can learn from. This will widen your perspectives toward life. When you embrace new outlooks toward life, you will likely become more empathetic toward others, as you'll have a better understanding of the reasons why they act or think in certain ways. This helps remove any prejudices that you may have had and creates more opportunities to work together with others for a common cause.

Stretch Your Limits

There are a variety of activities that you can engage in to give you more experience in taking risks. Here is an outline of some of them:

- **Volunteering:** You could start out by volunteering with groups that are aligned with what you love doing. This could be taking care of animals or activities that help to preserve the environment. This gives you greater experience that will surely be useful when you become an adult.
- **Get comfortable with crowds:** You may decide to participate in events that build your confidence, like public speaking, theatre performances, or singing. Learning to perform before crowds of people improves

your self-confidence and makes you relate much better with others.

- **Challenge your fears:** You could also decide to challenge your fears by doing things that you are normally frightened of. If you are scared of things like bungee jumping or zip-lining, you might need to try these. Exposing yourself to your fears and challenging them grows your ability to confront life's challenges and makes problem-solving easier for you. This may also prepare you for future leadership roles.
- **Take up responsibility:** You could also hone your management skills by accepting challenging community or school responsibilities. This improves your level of accountability, both to yourself and to those who look up to you for direction. As you expose yourself to new responsibilities, allow yourself to be open to criticism from those you engage with. Learn from positive feedback and constructive criticism while ignoring the negative feedback.

LEARNING FROM FAILURE

As a teenager, you are still in the process of establishing yourself based on new, unfamiliar experiences. You are more likely to make mistakes, but you can still rise up much better than you were before. Consider viewing mistakes as a chance for you to do things better the next time. Failures may also encourage you to engage with those who have different experiences from yours and get ideas from them. Accepting correction to improve on your mistakes and failures helps you to do things in a better way. Failures will also help you realize the inherent weaknesses that you were probably not aware of. When you become aware of your weaknesses, we encourage you to find someone to work together with who can complement your shortcomings instead of trying to do everything on your own.

Picking Up the Pieces

Starting all over again is often the most challenging thing to do after failing. However, after an encounter with failure, make time to reconsider what went wrong and develop better strategies to do better. It's important to note that you may not be able to completely avoid mistakes. If you encounter such cases, be at peace with some of the mistakes. Just be sure to develop skillful ways of limiting these mishaps each time. This will teach you to adjust and adapt so that you can move forward much better, even with imperfect work.

You will gradually develop a growth mindset that acknowledges mistakes. Such a mindset is positive and is often characterized by determination and perseverance. Such qualities will also serve as an inspiration and motivation to those around you. Realizing your limitations as you try out new things encourages you to celebrate every success, no matter how small they might appear to be.

MAKING WISE DECISIONS IN CHALLENGING SITUATIONS

The risks you take to improve yourself will surely pay off much later in your life. As a young, inexperienced teenager, one of the wisest decisions you could ever make is to find a mentor who guides you along. A mentor has likely faced most of the things that you are going through now and has overcome them at some point in their young life. Engaging them will save you time, as they are more likely to show you what works best for you based on their experience. Mentorship will also help you to create realistic goals. You may fancy certain things because of the way they are portrayed on TV or social media. However, in reality, those things may not quite be that way, and striving to attain them will eventually drain you. A mentor will highlight this to you on time so that you can save your effort and time by letting go of unrealistic ambitions.

Developing Personal Abilities

There are certain skills that you will have to develop on your own, even without the assistance of a mentor. Through your unique experiences, be sure to learn more about yourself and how you can respond to certain things in the future. Your personal preferences and priorities are things no mentor can help you with, so take charge of them. Listen to what your inner voice tells you, and trust your personal judgment. Be sure to practice mindfulness to maintain a clear mind so that you can make better decisions and perform effectively.

Develop the personal ability to pick the things that work for you while leaving out the things that don't. When you analyze things from a personal standpoint, you can easily weigh the consequences of your choices on your personal life without anybody else interfering with your decisions. The personal analysis also helps you to know when it's time to take a step back, rest, or completely let go of certain things. It allows you to put personal principles, beliefs, and priorities ahead of what might actually seem right to others but not to you.

This chapter took you through the importance of taking calculated risks for you to achieve the things you want. One of the things that can help you take calculated risks is seeking mentorship from more experienced individuals in areas that are desirable to you. Your personal experiences will also help you gain the courage to take calculated risks. As you make efforts to take calculated risks, you might encounter different people, including bullies. The next chapter looks at ways to help you deal with bullying.

4

BUSTING BULLIES

That awkward moment when someone asks, "What's wrong?" and they're the problem.

— ANONYMOUS

Nowadays, bullying occurs in various forms, most of which are very subtle, especially in schools. In such cases, the bullying cannot be easily identified, thereby preventing accountability and consequences on the part of the bullies. This clearly exposes the cowardice of bullying, considering that if it were noble and the bullies were proud of it, they would openly do it with no fear or shame whatsoever. This should be an encouragement to you as a victim of bullying, to let you know that you are a strong person, and the bully is actually the weak one. Like the previous chapter, this one also addresses the "resilience and grit" aspect of the B.R.A.V.E.S.T. framework.

Bullies naturally feel inferior, so they tend to try and make you feel the same, just so they can enjoy a sense of superiority. Their intention is to make you question your worth. This reminds me of the story "A War Not Won" by Dreyri Aldranaris (Aldranaris, 2023). In this story, a young and an old man are having a back-and-forth conversation. The older man, clearly in the "upper social class" in the eyes of the younger man, questions his junior on whether he is truly happy as an employee who only manages to get just enough to feed his dependents.

The young man is adamant that he is enjoying his life of making just enough to take care of his primary needs, even at the mercy of his superiors, who clearly don't value him that much. The dialogue continues, with the older man throwing in all the questions, all of which are responded to craftily by the young employee. It becomes apparent that the older man is only just trying to awaken his junior counterpart to the reality that he is actually a slave to a system.

At one point, the young employee is asked whether he would be truly happy to continue with the life he is living well into the future. The response that he gave was that there are many things in life that are more important than happiness. The young man says that as long as he is able to work, feed, eat, and maintain his home, he is fine. He says he really doesn't mind doing all he has to in order to please the people in power. He further alludes that, after all, those are the people who are intelligent and wise enough to make decisions that can serve people like him better. He even refers to himself as stupid and uneducated in this regard.

As the older man ends the conversation and leaves, the young man is left motionless in his worn-out shoes as he ponders hard on the dialogue. He looks to the sky, and tears fill his eyes. He acknowledged that what he had said in his conversation with the old man was a lie, just to keep him and his loved ones safe. The essence of the story is that, oftentimes, once you sustain an inferior mindset, it is likely that those you deem superior to you will keep exercising control over you. Bullies do just that. Once they ascertain that you think they are better than you, they will not stop making your life miserable.

DIFFERENT TYPES OF BULLYING

Bullying can occur in many different ways, usually depending on the level of interaction you have with the perpetrator. In cases where you are not close buddies, it is easier for you to immediately recognize bullying tendencies toward you and ward them off accordingly. This is usually the case with physical bullying. Bullying, however, becomes more difficult to deal with when the bully has some sort of close relationship with you. This is because you may initially think you are being overly sensitive. Let's delve into the various types of bullying that exist:

- **Relational bullying:** This type of bullying is closely aligned with emotional bullying, where your feelings are intentionally manipulated. Relational bullies take advantage of the relationship they have with you. As time progresses, your intimate association with the bully manipulates you into thinking that you are actually protecting the bully's feelings if you avoid confronting them over their behavior. This only perpetuates the bullying.

- **Indirect bullying:** In this case, the bully manipulates social situations by engaging in subtle actions that demean you. They may not directly attack you because of your closeness to them. A good example of this type of bullying is when a friend picks on you by making fun of something about you to indirectly offend you.

- **Disability bullying:** This is when bullies openly make fun of your physical disability. In other cases, they might deliberately ask you to perform a task they know you won't be able to fulfill because of your disability.

- **Sexual bullying:** Sexual bullying occurs when you have unwanted advances coming your way, even after making it clear that you don't appreciate them. It also includes nasty comments that are meant to get back at you for rejecting sexual advances.

- **Homophobic bullying:** This type is closely related to sexual bullying. In this case, you are specifically picked on because of your gender identity or sexual orientation. You should report all sexual or homophobic bullying immediately to your teachers, guardians, or authorities, as it often leads to aggression and violent attacks, which could harm you.

- **Verbal bullying:** When people say mean things to or about, you this is referred to as verbal bullying. It doesn't matter whether what is being said is true or not.

- **Cyberbullying:** This occurs when bullies use online platforms to pass demeaning and hurtful remarks behind the cover of digital media. This type of bullying includes social media bullying, where you are humiliated or threatened on common platforms like Twitter and Facebook, among others.

- **Racist bullying:** This is when abusive remarks are directed toward you because of your race.

BEHIND THE MASK

It is important to determine the reasons behind bullying. Most of the reasons behind bullying are usually centered on the need to control somebody else. This is because the bully often feels that they aren't in control of their own life. This can be a result of a troubled past of abuse and manipulation. Therefore, they may feel the need to inflict the same pain that they went through onto someone else. If you were to check the family background of most bullies, you would realize that some of them come from really troubled home environments.

The frustrations arising from not getting proper love and care from family usually make bullies develop the desire to control others and make the victims feel unworthy. In such instances, bullying is usually a way of venting out all the stored anger and resentment that they feel for the way they were treated. In broken homes and families, there is also a lack of accountability for one's unbecoming behavior in most cases. This often makes bullies think that their actions have no consequences for them to bear whatsoever.

Sometimes, bullies may even come from well-mannered families that do not condone bullying at all. However, just a personal lack of empathy or a misplaced belief in certain norms that encourage bullying makes them see it as a way of establishing authority over vulnerable people. Also, when someone wants to fit in with a group of kids they consider cool, they will likely do anything to please the members in exchange for acceptance. This meaningless need for validation often leads to bullying tendencies.

Nonetheless, instead of despising and resenting or even fearing bullies, your actions may actually be led by compassion toward them. Realizing that bullies need help with their behavior will help you cope better whenever you fall victim. You are not the problem; the bullies are. You shouldn't attribute the bullying to either your appearance or the way you carry yourself. At the same time, you should never seek to justify bullying by being fine with it.

The Hidden Wounds of Bullying

One of the major reasons bullying should be addressed immediately is that it has far-reaching consequences for the victims. In most cases, the bullies are perpetuating a cycle of the experiences that they have gone through. If care is not taken as a victim of bullying, you could end up also perpetuating the same cycle.

Some of the more pronounced effects of bullying are outlined here:

- **Reduced self-esteem:** Bullying may cause you to doubt your self-worth, resulting in social isolation. This often leads to chronic depression, among other issues like serious headaches and eating disorders.
- **Self-harm and suicidal thoughts:** These negative inclinations usually feed on isolation and loneliness, which also results from depression. Once you feel worthless, you are most likely to do those things, like substance abuse, that destroy both your body and purpose in life.
- **Poor social engagement:** This may cause you to disengage from activities that promote social interaction, thereby negatively affecting your ability to develop meaningful relationships with others. This will probably be because your ability to trust anybody becomes compromised. The more you distance yourself from relationships, however, the worse it gets for you. In the long term, you may develop conditions like Post Traumatic Stress Disorder (PTSD) or permanent psychological trauma. If your issues are left unresolved, these conditions will affect your career goals and overall life ambitions.

FROM VICTIM TO SURVIVOR

There are a variety of things that you can do to help yourself to recover from bullying. Some of the measures to take are outlined below:

- **Develop a positive mindset:** To recover from the negative effects of bullying, you need to recondition your mind to view yourself as a victor, not a victim. Bullying thrives on a damaged mental cycle. In order to break free from it for good, accept that your bullied past cannot be relived and undone. However, it is possible for you to regain power over your life. This has a calming effect on your mind and helps to remove the feelings of unworthiness.
- **Forgive the bully and let go of resentment:** Make efforts to let go of any resentment you may feel toward your bully so that you can better live in the present. Once you are clear from the bullying experiences, seek external support from friends and professional counselors. This will help you map the way forward much easier.
- **Assert your boundaries:** You should develop the ability to boldly say no to bullies. When your resolve is firm, bullies are less likely to bother you. These are weak people who can only have their way if you allow them to.
- **Document the instances of bullying:** It is important to remember to keep a record of all the evidence of bullying, including text messages. This makes it easier

to report and resolve cases of being bullied. You could also deliberately allow a bully to have their way over you while a friend secretly records video and audio footage of the encounter. This surely nails the bully, without a doubt.

- **Participate in awareness campaigns against bullying:** Doing this helps you to develop better strategies for dealing with bullying in the future. With a strong support base of friends and peers, you will find it easier to manage it.

- **Play smart:** At times, the best way to prevent bullying is to avoid it altogether by playing smart. Do not participate in heated verbal exchanges with bullies. Bullies are often calculative and will usually create an enabling environment that favors their bullying intentions. In other cases where confrontation is inevitable, you could also act smart by engaging with the bully in a calm dialogue that promotes resolution. This will likely pacify the situation, as sometimes bullies may subconsciously yearn for someone to talk to who can understand them without passing judgment.

ONLINE WARRIORS

As a teen, you probably spend a reasonable amount of your time on social media. These platforms are good for networking and socializing. They can, however, be easily manipulated by bullies. Most bullies hide behind fake social media identities to carry out their intentions without leaving an obvious trace.

Some of the effective ways to avoid such people are described below:

- **Activate your privacy settings**: Activating your account's privacy settings helps to limit the accessibility of your personal information on social media. You could also activate your privacy settings to prevent unknown accounts from viewing your personal details altogether.
- **Limit your use of social media:** You could create a schedule for visiting social media that you stick to. This regulates the time you spend online, thereby lowering your chances of sharing unnecessary information that the bullies could use against you. If you notice that someone has bullying tendencies, remove them from your friend list altogether. Block them if they pester you for reconnection with them.
- **Improve your security settings:** This limits the chances of cyberbullies tampering with your account. Create a very strong password and activate two-factor authentication to minimize the chances of your account being hacked.
- **Take overall charge:** Also, taking better overall control over the content you post and the conversations you engage in with strangers on common social media platforms will reduce your chances of crossing paths with online bullies.

Bullying among teens takes many different forms, which include physical, emotional, sexual, and cyberbullying, among other types. Bullies will usually pick on their victims to project their own insecurities so that they gain a feeling of superiority over them. The best way to deal with bullying is to prevent it from happening in the first place by being assertive and refusing to act on the command of bullies. Remember to always report bullying to the responsible authorities, either at your school or community, whenever it occurs. Having said this, you need some survival tips with regard to school. Check out the school survival guide in the next chapter.

5

SCHOOL SURVIVAL GUIDE

 I think school and microwave minutes are longer than regular minutes.

— ALBERT EINSTEIN

Most teenagers do not like school days, especially when having difficulties in grasping concepts. The story "Growing Down" by Shel Silverstein can help you if you are also failing to grasp taught concepts. There was a man called Brown who always ended up telling boys and girls to grow up. Nearly every issue would end up with a "Grow up!" and this earned him the nickname "Grow-Up Brown." At some point, the teenagers decided to do the opposite by asking him to grow down. He then tried to grow down by doing silly things like climbing trees, crawling on his knees, yelling, and jumping, among other things that kids do. Brown ended up enjoying the idea of growing down. If Brown was flexible enough to learn to grow down, you could also possibly navigate through academic needs and responsibilities. Continue to develop your "resilience and grit" using this chapter.

STUDY SMARTER, NOT HARDER

Studying habits and note-taking skills are not acquired naturally. You should learn how to develop study habits so that your educational journey becomes easier. Please note that there is no one-size-fits-all approach when it comes to learning how to effectively study. Here are some general strategies that can help you study smarter.

Create a Designated Study Space

Your studying space should be free from noise to avoid distractions. Make sure gadgets like your cell phone and television are away from your study room. If there are enough rooms, your study room should be far from the sitting one so that the family members will not disturb you when conversing and having fun.

Your studying environment should be motivating enough to encourage you to work. The room should be tidy and well-organized. The books, calculators, and other stationery should be easily accessible. You can also consider adding some houseplants that can beautify the room while freshening up the air.

Break Study Sessions Into Manageable Chunks

Studying does not mean that you have to spend the whole day scrolling through your curriculum. You should also have time to rest and have fun with friends and your family. Too much work without rest can make you unproductive. You should create a study timetable and indicate the time to spend on every subject or module. A break after every session is also necessary to rejuvenate yourself so that you avoid memory fatigue. Consider allocating more time to the subject that is more challenging to you.

Use Active Learning Techniques

Active learning techniques can help you enhance your understanding and retention of information. This approach involves discussing concepts with your colleagues, summarizing information, and participating in hands-on activities. Using mnemonic devices can also assist you in recalling information more effectively. In this case, you use techniques like creating vivid mental images, visualization, and acronyms.

You can also use mind-mapping techniques to connect and organize ideas using maps or diagrams that show the relationships between the concepts. The spaced repetition technique is also effective if you are trying to retain some information for a long period of time. You should space out your study sessions over time instead of cramming all the concepts in at once. You can also retain and recall information easily by self-testing and using quizzes. This will strengthen your memory, and you can better identify areas that need further review.

Establish a Study Routine

Having a consistent schedule can help you to be more productive by following set study times. So, you should set the studying times based on your energy levels and personal preferences. For you not to lose track of your schedule, introduce tools like planners, study applications, or calendars. These will act as reminders by setting alarms or notifications so that you may not miss any activity or due dates for assignments.

Seek Help From Others

When you encounter challenges, don't hesitate to ask your teachers or peers. Reaching out to others for help could be the best strategy to enhance a better understanding of the taught concepts. Seeking clarification on difficult tasks shows commitment to your studies. You may get the answers to many questions or get additional resources to overcome the problems at hand. You can also engage in group discussions with your peers so that you can share ideas.

MANAGING EXAM STRESS

High school learners usually have end-of-year examinations. It is normal for you to have mixed feelings as they become stressed by examinations while they are also happy about wrapping up the year. Moderate exam stress is good as it can improve your performance and alertness and boost your memory. Stress can be easily managed if you are resilient and confident that you can manage it. It can be overwhelming if you also have negative energy toward it. In most cases, stress can encourage you to deal with threatening tasks. Let's go through some coping techniques that you might find handy.

Practice Deep Breathing

You can reduce stress or anxiety during exams by introducing relaxation techniques like breathing exercises. Make sure you choose a comfortable position, be it standing, sitting, or lying down. Then, close your eyes and take a minute to relax your body by releasing any tension in your muscles. You can then use your nose to slowly breathe in to fill your lungs with air and allow your abdomen to expand. Then, use your mouth to breathe out, but make sure you exhale the air in a steady and controlled way.

Get Ample Sleep the Night Before Exams

Getting ample sleep the night before exams is crucial for optimizing focus and concentration. When you sleep, your brain refreshes itself, boosts memory, and integrates information for perfect mental performance. You can achieve this by establishing a sleep routine. You can set your alarm so that you can sleep and wake up at the same time every day.

To sleep well, make sure the environment is conducive. The room should be dark, comfortable, and quiet for you to relax.

You can use eye masks, white noise machines, or earplugs to minimize interruptions. Be sure to avoid caffeine, sugary drinks or foods, and nicotine when it is nearly time to sleep. You should stay away from using electrical devices like tablets, computers, or smartphones for at least an hour before going to bed, as they can disturb your natural sleep-wake cycle.

Motivate Yourself

You should ask for guidance and encouragement from your teachers, peers, and family members. They can assist you to build confidence and believe in yourself. They can help you to be able to utilize positive self-talk. You will be able to cheerlead yourself by saying positive statements like "I have what it takes to succeed," or "I got this."

You can also boost confidence by reviewing your past exam successes. This will motivate you to keep pushing so that you do better than the past exam. Self-belief can make you focus on your progress and limit comparing yourself with other teenagers.

Eat a Balanced Diet

You should stay hydrated and have a balanced diet so that your brain can function properly. Your overall well-being and everyday functioning are determined by the brain, as it is the core center of the nervous system. You should keep it healthy and active.

THE BALANCING ACT

As a teenager, life can be overwhelming, and you may fail to balance school and personal activities. There are effective strategies that can help you to manage, some of which are listed in this section.

- **Manage your time:** You should learn to manage your time by creating a schedule. Prioritize tasks according to their urgency and importance, as mentioned earlier in this chapter.
- **Communicate your commitments:** Communication is important to avoid conflicts among people. You should notify your family or friends about your commitments. They will not bother you with other activities when they know your schedule. As teenagers, usually, friends can tempt you to ignore your schedule and accompany them to socializing tasks. You should learn to say "no" if you are to maintain a healthy balance.
- **Practice delegation:** You should delegate some tasks when necessary to lessen your burden of responsibilities. This can also help you to have time for breaks and downtime to relax. For example, let your younger siblings do the dishes while you are cooking.
- **Seek support from people around you:** If you feel overwhelmed, seek support from your family, mentors, or teachers. You should vent out if the pressure is too much or if you feel stressed. They will comfort and advise you on how best to go around issues regarding your studies.

- **Incorporate enjoyable activities:** Too much work without rest can make you feel exhausted and become unproductive. You should also do enjoyable activities to rejuvenate the brain, but they should be in line with your hobbies and personal interests.

As a teenager, you should note that studying harder can sometimes not produce the desired results. You should work smarter by doing all that is necessary for a successful learning process. Know the techniques to involve, like developing schedules, using technological tools, and being positive about yourself. Although school work is important, social life is crucial too. Balancing the two assists you in avoiding stress, which can cause more harm than good to the human brain. Mind you, stress is one of the triggers for substance abuse, which is further discussed in the next chapter.

6

SUBSTANCE SMARTS

If you ran like your mouth, you'd be in good shape!

— ANONYMOUS

Getting high is pretty cool to imagine, especially as a teen who's only heard about others' experiences. No doubt, your personal experiences usually turn out to be your best life teachers. However, with substance abuse, the best lessons will likely come with some not-so-pleasant experiences. Your income sources as a teen are surely limited and certainly not enough to sustain a life of getting regularly hooked on illicit substances. It reminds me of the funny "Thank you Ma'am" story by Langston Hughes. In the story, a young teen called Roger tries to snatch Mrs. Luella Bates Washington Jones' pocketbook down an alley toward midnight. The tiny boy fails to grip his targeted snatch, and the huge woman grabs him by the collar. She drags Roger to her home while the little boy appears so frightened, not knowing what the lady would do with him. She inquires of him why he would attempt such a disgraceful thing of trying to snatch her pocketbook, to which he responds that he only wanted money to buy himself a pair of suede shoes.

At her home, she instructs him to wash up and goes further to prepare him a sumptuous meal. Afterward, the unexpected happens. She hands Roger ten dollars to buy the blue suede shoes he so desires and instructs him to leave, which leaves the teenager speechless. At last, he could only manage the words "Thank you, ma'am." Now, Roger's encounter is funny, but sadly true for most teens who live hooked on various substances. Chances are high that you may not be as fortunate as Roger, and things may end up not looking too good for you. You will certainly need "resilience and grit" from the B.R.A.V.E.S.T. framework to escape the pangs of substance abuse.

FROM PILLS TO PUFFS

This section takes you through some of the most common substances that are taken by teens to feel high. The instant temporary effects of the "high" are described for each substance while also highlighting the drawbacks and either short or long-term effects of each.

- **Alcohol:** The minimum legal drinking age in America is 21. As a teen, it is illegal for you to purchase alcohol. Aside from the legal implications, alcohol intake increases your chances of being involved in wrong drunken behaviors, like harming your friends, destroying school or home property, and obscene sexual activity, among others.

- **Marijuana:** Marijuana causes your teen brain, which is still developing, to encounter difficulties in memorizing academic tasks. You will find it hard to concentrate and solve basic problems that you would ordinarily manage. Marijuana also affects your body's coordination, making it difficult to engage in activities that require teamwork, which include sports or constructive group work in class.
- **Tobacco and nicotine:** Smoking cigarettes exposes you to nicotine, which affects your tender brain tissue that is still developing. This compromises your overall thinking abilities when completing tasks that you are given in class. It also results in poor athletic capabilities since tobacco affects your lungs and, hence, your breathing abilities. Tobacco can also cause a nasty cough in teens, in addition to heart and eye problems, not to mention unsightly yellow teeth.
- **Prescription medications:** Misusing prescription drugs such as cough syrups or opiate painkillers could cause permanent damage to your body. Overdoses of these drugs may cause serious health complications that could negatively affect your life forever.
- **Inhalants:** Inhalants are popular among teens because they bring drunkenness relatively quicker than other substances. Aerosols and solvents are the most common inhalants, which cause confusion and deep drowsiness.

Staggering and dizziness may follow, posing risks of falling over and hurting yourself, in addition to damaging valuables at school or home. Inhalants could also damage your sense of smell or cause nosebleeds.

- **Stimulants:** Stimulants artificially increase the feelings of good sensations throughout your body. However, stimulant abuse also affects your blood circulation, thereby negatively impacting your breathing. Stimulants also cause a rapid increase in body temperature, resulting in fatigue and possibly fainting. They also increase your chances of developing seizures in extreme cases. Your nervous system may also become unnaturally reactive, causing cycles of excitement and depression in extreme extents.

- **Hallucinogens:** Hallucinogens cause you to see imaginary things that others cannot, thereby disconnecting you from the reality of your surroundings. This is risky, as it compromises your ability to see and avoid danger. You may end up making decisions that you think are good, yet they actually harm you and those around you. Large doses can cause flashbacks of nasty events, in addition to vomiting and stomach pain.

- **Opioids:** Opioids like heroin can cause your brain to be clouded with confusing thoughts while also triggering drowsiness and constipation. This causes poor academic performance and antisocial attributes that will likely push your friends away from you. You may also end up neglecting your appearance, making you look untidy.

- **Club drugs:** Club drugs are meant to hype your mood at parties so that you artificially seem to enjoy the experience even more. These drugs include magic mushrooms, ecstasy, PCP (commonly known as angel dust), and LSD (popularly known as mellow yellow). They affect your coordination, memory, and judgment, increasing your likelihood of making really bad decisions. They also stimulate your body functions, increasing heart rate and blood pressure.

- **Synthetic cannabinoids:** Manmade cannabinoids cause extensive detachment from reality by inducing deep hallucinations. These drugs cause dangerous behavior in teens, resulting from deep delusions about what's happening around you. They cause extremes of both euphoric feelings and severe withdrawal from your friends and family.

- **Synthetic cathinones:** Commonly known as bath salts, these drugs actually have nothing to do with bathing but everything to do with artificial body stimulation. Teens usually mix these drugs with juice or food, while in other cases, the substances can be taken by snorting or injecting. They increase the levels of the feel-good hormone dopamine, making you euphoric. Abuse of these substances causes violent disposition, anxiety, loss of appetite, and muscle spasms, among other symptoms.

- **Over-the-counter (OTC) medications:** Abusing over-the-counter medications can cause dehydration and damage to internal organs like kidneys and the liver. Teens take them to experience a high that is usually short-lasting. The drugs are readily available, and anyone can purchase them anywhere; hence, teens often overlook their dangers.

THE PRICE OF SUBSTANCE ABUSE

Substance abuse brings you many problems that will likely overwhelm you as a young person, considering that some of your vital organs are still developing. Your main focus is your schoolwork, and that's the area that is mostly affected by abusing these substances. Good class performance requires a clear mind, which can be compromised by substance abuse. Substance abuse strains your relationships with your loved ones. This is because you won't be able to communicate on the same basis of sanity anymore. Your social life will thus be greatly affected, making you an outcast, alienated from your friends, family, and community. Your teen years are the most critical in shaping the life that you want to live. Substance abuse may lead to poor grades, which may further hinder you from attaining higher qualifications that are needed to follow the career that you desire.

Illegal recreational substances are also quite expensive to get. As a teen, you surely have limited income, making it difficult to sustain a life on these drugs. This may expose you to unbecoming behavior like inappropriate sexual activity and crime just to sustain the lifestyle. Ultimately, continued use may cause your health to deteriorate, mainly due to internal organ damage. This can also further impair your ability to make sound decisions on schoolwork and social life, thereby pushing you to chronic anxiety and depression. You may then likely find no motivation in living a purposeful life, especially with poor class grades that paint a bleak picture of potential career prospects. With nothing left to hold on to, you may likely slip into long-term substance dependency and, ultimately, addiction, which could have fatal effects on your social, emotional, psychological, and physical well-being.

NATURAL HIGHS

Your fascination with thrilling activities that keep you on the edge will surely peak during your adolescence. In other words, teenage years are associated with a state of becoming naturally high. You are at a stage where you are experiencing new things that naturally come with the joy of being a "first-timer." After the initial fascination wears off, the temptation to take substances that give you a sense of reliving those good experiences may arise. The "high" that you will experience is an artificial one, based on a fallacy, which will soon wear off, leaving you feeling worse than you initially felt. Nonetheless, did you know that you could experience such "highs" continuously if you so wished, without the need for mood-altering substances? You may begin by creating a circle of friends whose presence really gives you joy. While doing so, remember to keep away from the bad associations that disturb your peace.

As you continue to explore more natural ways of experiencing highs, you will develop the energy that will propel you to pursue your passions. This way, you can unleash your creativity and full potential. Making the healthy choice to focus on experiencing natural highs aligns you with your true self and with a strong social life around positively minded people. This atmosphere helps you grow academically, in sports, or in any hobbies. Your mind and body also respond positively to natural highs. Where you would probably have encountered withdrawal symptoms from abusing substances to achieve a high, the natural strategies help you to experience euphoric feelings continuously with no side effects. Isn't that a wonderful prospect to consider? It's certainly worth giving a try!

SAFE HAVENS

You may have been experimenting with illegal substances and consequently made some really bad decisions. Does that spell the end of the road for you? Absolutely not; rest assured of that. We all have made terrible decisions we are not proud of at some point, but we still managed to find our way back, much stronger and more resilient. You may not be too sure how, but don't worry yourself. The help you need is right within your reach. You could start by talking with your school counselors for guidance and counseling. These highly trained professionals know their job and will not leak a word to your school teachers, friends, or family. Their desire is to help you stop taking the bad stuff and see you succeed in your life. Please note that the counselors are not there to judge or condemn you. You may also prefer to join support groups that bring together other teens who may be dealing with similar substance abuse issues. You are bound to feel embraced, being around positively minded people like you, who have similarly decided to turn their lives around for the better.

In some extreme cases where your addiction has really gone too far, you may have to involve your family so that they engage trained medical professionals and therapists. They surely desire to see you at your best, so you need not be ashamed at all. Professional therapy is likely to get you on the recovery path much quicker so that you can focus on your school and career dreams sooner. Nonprofit organizations will also be quite helpful for your recovery, as their goal isn't to get anything from you but rather to help you get your real self back. These organizations are particularly helpful in times when they engage other recovering adults to help motivate you to do the same. Building trust and connection with such mentors, who have walked a similar path as you have, gives you greater control and accountability over your life choices going forward. This will improve your genuine commitment to kicking substance abuse out of your life for good.

Being smart enough to keep away from artificial highs that are caused by substance abuse is the main focus of this chapter. The different substances teens normally crave for them to get high were covered in this chapter, together with their long and short-term effects on users. Natural ways of achieving similar highs to those induced by substance abuse were recommended. These are the ideal ways of coping with the craving to get high, which is common in many teens. Additionally, safe corrective measures and resorts were proposed, which included professional counseling to get substance abusers back on track. The next chapter focuses on how you can embrace change as a teenager.

7

TRANSITIONS

While still in school, you are probably envisioning a certain future for yourself with a specific environment in mind. You probably fancy the lifestyle your role model has, and you aspire to be just like them one day. True, your future will likely need a different version of you in a new environment. However, it is highly unlikely that the exact physical environment that you dream of being in in the future will be the actual one that you will occupy. Desiring an ideal future life is a good aspiration to have, but it requires a radical shift in the way you think, speak, and do things. You might even need a change in your environment. Once you do that, you will change the way you see things, and your life will transform accordingly. Please note that this chapter contributes to the "A" part of the B.R.A.V.E.S.T. framework, which stands for "accept and adapt to change."

THE BEAUTY OF CHANGING YOUR ENVIRONMENT

Your future becomes much clearer and more aligned with your purpose, passion, and abilities when you change your environment. The elegance of change is expressed wonderfully in the poem "Echoe of Nature's Beauty" by Zuhaib Ali (Ali, 2023). The writer illustrates their longing for nature's embrace by wandering through its tranquil beauty. The expression "new dreams ensuing where the forests are green" highlights the ability of your environment to change the way you think. Your body changes significantly during adolescence. This is often accompanied by changes in your preferences for various psychological and physical needs, including the desire to alter your surroundings. This shows that change is inevitable. However, you can direct the changes that you want to see in your life in many ways that are outlined in this chapter.

Rolling With Uncertainty

New environments are often accompanied by transitioning to a new person altogether. You need ample time to adjust to that new life. You also need to prepare your mind well prior to the transition. A positive mind anticipates the best outcome from the change of environment and helps you to adapt much easier. Learning to cope with these radical shifts will ultimately develop your resilience and ability to manage the stress that is associated with adapting to new and unfamiliar environments.

Things to Expect in a New Environment

Once you embrace change as an opportunity for personal development, you will realize the following:

- You will start discovering new dimensions of yourself that you probably weren't aware of.
- You may start losing interest in some of the things that you previously loved doing while also developing a desire to try new things out.
- Your circle of friends will change to align with your new activities and routine.

Things That Will Help You to Easily Adapt to a Change in Environment

Here are some of the things that will make your transition into the new environment much easier:

- **Strong support network:** During this time, you will need a strong network of family and friends who support and encourage you to embrace the change.
- **A healthy body:** Remember to take good care of your body by eating healthy food, drinking plenty of water, exercising, and resting well. This is because changes in the routine and nature of your activities may put a physical strain on your body, which you would need to manage well.
- **Mentorship**: A mentor may also be necessary to help you manage the change. Mentorship helps you to adjust

quicker to the new self you are becoming by providing proven strategies that support change. This will usually be based on the mentor's personal experiences with handling change.

- **Set realistic targets:** When your physical environment changes, other areas of your life will naturally require adjustments. This shows that change is a process that will take considerable time for you to get everything in place. You should be realistic about the timeframes that you set for yourself. For example, you may decide to completely let go of a certain activity for good and adopt, say, a new hobby instead. This may require you to develop new relationships, which will surely take a while, so you will have to be patient with yourself.

THE ENVIRONMENT SHUFFLE

A change in the environment is usually accompanied by a shift in the way you do things. In this section, we highlight some of the things that you should do to help you cope better with your new environment:

- **Keep a positive mind:** This allows you to believe in the change and understand why it is necessary. Keeping a positive mind also helps you to endure the challenges that you will meet along the way.
- **Realize the limitations of your old environment:** This helps you to be proud of your new surroundings as you transition into a different person. Support your

decision to change by utilizing new opportunities and resources in your new environment.

- **Join social peer groups in your new environment:** Peer groups are a platform where new relationships can be fostered. Be willing to genuinely connect with new people by valuing cultural diversity and embracing new perspectives with an open mind. As you meet new people, remember to stay true to your personal purpose and identity.

- **Seek advice:** New environments usually may present routines and expectations that you are unfamiliar with. Take time out to familiarize yourself by seeking guidance from those who are well-versed with the norms, such as counselors or teachers. Sporting events, cultural groups, and social gatherings are usually good places to initiate conversations and meet new people who may give you advice on how to go about certain things.

- **Develop curiosity:** As you explore your new surroundings, ask questions whenever you can. Be inquisitive on the matters that fascinate you while giving out the knowledge that you also have on unique matters.

FRIENDSHIP REMIX

Approaching location changes with an open mind fosters new connections. However, establishing relationships using those connections takes some time. There are a few things you may need to consider for you to build strong friendships:

- **Establish common ground:** You will need to identify common interests and focus on them first before committing to a lasting friendship.
- **Be authentic:** Being your true self increases your chances of meeting new people who align with your interests. This makes it easier to establish genuine friendships.
- **Be open and truthful:** As you begin interacting with new people, communicate honestly and respectfully so that you can build trust. If people trust you, they are more likely to be more open and reveal their true selves to you.
- **Spend more time together with new connections:** This helps to build familiarity, which is the foundation of any bonds that you can develop with new friends. Sharing the different experiences of where you are coming from may also help to identify common ground, while creating new experiences together will deepen your friendships.
- **Show respect and be supportive**: It will be good for you to respect the beliefs, traditions, and cultures of everyone you meet, even if you are not necessarily friends with them. Simply put, be inclusive. Supporting and respecting others will encourage them to do the same for you in return, which could mark the beginning of new friendships. Allow friendships to happen naturally without pushing people's boundaries. Once a friendship is established, do everything possible to cherish the relationship for you to build lifelong connections.

- **Accept that not everyone will connect with you:** It is the desire of most teens to feel included and be popular. However, the truth is that not everyone is going to like you or regard you the way you expect. Some people will just not vibe with you, not because they dislike you, but because they have different preferences. This is a somewhat bitter truth to bear, but the sooner you come to terms with it, the easier it will be for you to build real friendships. As such, you should not try to force yourself onto people, as doing so actually violates their freedom of association. Likewise, you, too, will need to put down firm boundaries around the things you like and those you wouldn't appreciate.

This chapter has looked at what happens when you change your environment as a teenager and the things you may do for you to adapt easily. Accept reality and adopt a positive mindset. Be willing to develop new connections based on common interests. Consider being outgoing and engaging in honest conversations with new people to build genuine trust and, ultimately, lasting friendships. It is also important to familiarize yourself with your new environment so that you can understand the culture and norms before adjusting accordingly. While adapting to changes in your environment is important, you also need to familiarize yourself with changes that happen to your body. This is why the next chapter will address accepting and adapting to puberty.

8

HORMONES, ZITS, AND GROWTH SPURTS

Even as kids reach adolescence, they need more than
ever for us to watch over them. Adolescence is not about
letting go. It's about hanging on during a difficult time.

— RON TAFFEL

Puberty is a time during which physical, emotional, and psychological changes happen in the body of a growing child as a result of changes in hormone production. Puberty is better described as the process through which the body matures into adulthood, developing an ability for sexual reproduction. This is possibly a very difficult time for a teenager, which is why you need a lot of knowledge. During puberty, your emotions may become much stronger while your body rapidly changes physically. This usually happens between eight and 14 years of age and beyond, but the specific changes differ with each individual. Please note that puberty is an ongoing process that comes in stages and can span over years.

The more educated and aware of what to expect you are, the less weird and stressful puberty will be. In most cases, children will feel anxious and confused, but if you talk to your parents or others you can trust, it will be much easier. The good thing is that every adult has been through puberty, so they better understand what you are going through. This chapter fully explains what happens during puberty and how to deal with some of the unexpected changes that come with it. This chapter will explore the inner changes that happen during puberty while still addressing the "A" part of the B.R.A.V.E.S.T. framework.

SHAPE-SHIFTING SHENANIGANS

The adjustment into adulthood comes with growth and changes in the body that most teenagers may find difficult to deal with. It is key for you to know that puberty is a normal part of growing up and can be embraced with ease. Here are some of the changes that you can expect in your body as you go through puberty:

- **Rapid growth spurts and changes in height and body proportions:** During puberty, you suddenly grow taller. For boys, the chest and shoulders become broader, and muscle mass increases. Girls may find themselves putting on more weight, with the body becoming more defined and curvy. The weight fluctuations may also be attributed to the increase in appetite that comes with puberty. The voices of boys deepen as vocal cords grow.

- **Development of primary sexual characteristics:** This stage comes with the maturation of sexual reproductive organs as well as potential fertility. For boys, your penis and your testicles get bigger. For some, they may experience some swelling around the nipples, which may appear like they are beginning to grow breasts. This, however, then goes away. For girls, breasts get bigger, and you may also start getting your menstrual period, which can be irregular at the beginning. Your labia may also change in color and start to grow bigger.

- **Appearance of secondary sexual characteristics:** Facial hair begins to develop in boys. You begin to grow pubic hair, which is basically hair that grows around your genitals. The hair can begin to grow on other parts of the body, like armpits, arms, and legs. This hair grows darker and will be more noticeable as time progresses.

- **Changes in body odor and increased oil production:** As you enter puberty, your body begins to sweat more as regulation of body temperature changes. Body odor becomes an inevitable issue at this point. This may require you to adjust your shower routine and start using deodorants. During puberty, you may develop acne, which is caused by increased oil production, and this can appear on your face or body.

A STORM OF EMOTIONS

There are different ways in which the emotional and psychological changes of puberty manifest. The most common is a change of behavior. The way teens respond and deal with this emotional adjustment varies, though a difference from their normal behavior is usually notable.

- **Heightened self-consciousness and awareness of body image:** It is quite normal to be self-conscious about the changes that are happening to your body. It can be very difficult for you to deal with the changes in your body at the same time you are trying to fit in with your friends (Nivedita, 2019). Your self-esteem and self-confidence can fluctuate rapidly because of physical changes in your body.
- **Intensified emotional sensitivity and susceptibility to mood swings:** The intensity of your emotions heightens during puberty. You feel a lot of things at once in your environment, within yourself, and with your relationships. As a result, your emotions are turned up very high, and you will likely find yourself to be irritable or sad at the pettiest of things. You should be gentle on yourself and take some time alone whenever you need to. You should also start learning to communicate positively and constructively to manage your emotions better. In some extreme cases, you may consider professional help to assist with managing your emotions.

- **Increased desire for independence and autonomy from parental influence:** Most teenagers begin to explore their uniqueness as individuals. As a result, they find themselves wanting to associate more with their friends than with their parents and families. During this stage, conflict is likely to happen between you and your parents as you struggle to be independent. You should, therefore, try as much as possible to become a unique individual within the confines of your parents' guidance.

- **Heightened interest in forming romantic and intimate relationships:** As you develop physically and emotionally, you also reach sexual maturity. You will find yourself becoming curious about sex and will begin to become attracted to other people (Menstrupedia, 2019). It is during puberty that you begin to have "crushes," infatuations, and emotional attachments. Your sexuality emerges, and everything you feel is very normal.

- **Development of empathy and increased understanding of others' emotions:** The changes in the puberty-related emotions of teenagers may lead them to become more understanding and have more empathy for others. If this happens, you also reach emotional and cognitive maturation, and this sharpens your decision-making ability. Your judgment of what is good and bad becomes clearer, and you attain a more considerate approach toward the consequences of your behavior and actions.

ZIT HAPPENS

One of the most common occurrences during puberty is acne, commonly referred to as zits or pimples. Your body will be experiencing hormonal changes, and this, in turn, leads to increased oil production. You then develop acne, which tends to negatively affect the self-esteem of most teenagers. Here are tips for dealing with acne:

- **Regularly cleanse your face with gentle products to manage acne:** You should find products that are gentle for your skin type and use them to cleanse your skin and get rid of the excess oil. Typically, products that contain benzoyl peroxide or salicylic acid as the main ingredients are good. Use noncomedogenic skincare products to avoid clogging pores. Always cleanse and rinse your face with lukewarm water for best results. Alternatively, you can consult a dermatologist for recommendations on personalized acne treatment options.
- **Avoid touching or picking at acne:** The more you pick at the acne, the more damage is done to the skin. This eventually leads to scarring when the acne clears. This is yet another problem that you will have to deal with.
- **Consider wearing minimal makeup:** Doing this helps your skin to breathe more. You should try as much as possible not to clog your pores, as this holds oil and dirt under your skin, thereby increasing the chances of more outbreaks. Avoid excessive sun exposure and use oil-free, noncomedogenic sunscreen.

FUNK-FREE REVOLUTION

The increased sweat production that comes with puberty causes more body odor. One funny thing, however, is that you may not even be able to know that you stink unless someone else tells you. Relax a bit as you go through this short story called "The Foolish Fish."

Once upon a time, there lived many fish in a huge pond. These fish were arrogant and would never take advice. Along with them lived a very kind crocodile. He always advised the fish that it was not good to be too confident and arrogant. In turn, they would mock him and claim that he did not mind his own business. One day, two fishermen stopped by the pond to drink water. One of them said that the pond had many fish, and they agreed to come back the following morning to cast their nets. The crocodile overhead them, and he went straight to warn the fish. "You'd better leave this pond," he warned. The fish were adamant, claiming that many fishermen had tried to catch them but had not been successful. The crocodile let them be. The following day, the fishermen came and cast their nets. Soon, all the fish were caught. "If only we had listened to the crocodile," they said. For their arrogance, they had to pay with their lives. Hopefully, you won't get annoyed when others let you know how bad you might be smelling. After all, it's reversible if you follow these tips:

- **Shower regularly and use antibacterial soap to control body odor:** Your body produces more sweat, so you need to shower more, too (Nersesian, 2021). Make it a point to wear clean clothes after showering. This includes having a clean change of underwear and socks to maintain freshness. After showering, always use antiperspirant to manage the underarm odor.

- **Keep your living space clean and well-ventilated to minimize odors:** Always make sure your room is clean and well-ventilated. Make it a daily routine to make your bed and open windows. You should also change your linen periodically to avoid holding body odor on your bed. Consider using room sprays and diffusers to alleviate odors and keep your space smelling nice.
- **Consider using natural remedies:** You can add baking soda or lemon to your bath water to alleviate strong body odor. In the case that the odor is too strong and does not seem to go away, consider consulting a doctor.
- **Practice good oral hygiene:** Bad breath is just as disturbing as body odor, and you need to do away with it. Make use of oral hygiene products like mouthwash and dental floss to complement your normal oral care routine.

TLC FOR THE TEEN SOUL

Puberty is a part of human development that no one can evade. As such, it is always best to embrace the changes that are happening to you. It is important to appreciate your uniqueness and take good care of yourself. Despite the changes, always celebrate your body and focus on its goodness rather than what you think is bad about it. Here are some pointers to help you embrace puberty:

- **Find healthy ways to manage stress and cope with emotional ups and downs:** One of the best ways is to keep yourself busy. Find a hobby or physical activity likea sport that you can do. This helps you to focus on the good side of life as you go through the puberty stage. Also, engage in self-reflection to give yourself time to explore your passions and personal interests.

- **Seek support from trusted adults or mentors for guidance and understanding:** Make sure you have all the support you can get from trusted adults. You should also embrace open communication with family and friends about your experiences.

- **Educate yourself about puberty to dispel myths and ease concerns:** There are so many myths about the changes that happen to teens during puberty. Try to educate yourself as much as possible, as this eases your journey and makes you realize that you are normal.

- **Practice good hygiene habits to take care of your changing body:** It is very beneficial to take care of yourself during puberty. Good hygiene practices are essential. The changes happening in your body may require you to adjust your self-care routine and be more vigilant. In all this, be patient with yourself and remember that this is a natural process.

Puberty is a natural process that you should not be afraid of. It comes with various changes in the body, and these differ for boys and girls. It is very important to be emotionally prepared. The next chapter will focus on visualizing and developing positivity, which is also very important as you transition into adulthood.

9

DREAM IT, SEE IT, BE IT

My mother always told me if you can't say anything nice, then don't say anything at all...And some people wonder why I'm so quiet around them.

— ANONYMOUS

Your teenage years can be the most exciting time of your life. Guess why? Yeah, you are slowly becoming who you want to be. You can become all you have always dreamed of being. Those famous TV personalities, cool singers, and stylish celebrities you see every day were once your age at some point. They also went through the same things that you are experiencing now. You, too, can become just like any one of them and accomplish even more, but it all begins in your mind. If you keep your mind focused on that lifestyle that you desire for your adult years, it will surely come true. All you have to do is to keep believing that you are already on the journey toward that life.

Adolescence can also be a very confusing time for you, with many important decisions and choices to make. Your desires for the future may not match your family circumstances, making your dreams appear challenging. You may feel dejected because others seem to find their way through life much easier. They come from well-to-do families that give them all they want, like nice clothes, the latest video games, and cool vacations at expensive resorts, while some even get cars as gifts from their parents. It's understandable to feel that way. When you consider the other side of life, though, you probably won't spend a second longer worried about your situation anymore. Someone else out there is dreaming of the very things you have. As such, expressing gratitude for those things you have at the moment will help you enjoy your present life as you prepare for a better one. This chapter is the only one that addresses the "V" part of the B.R.A.V.E.S.T. framework, which looks at "visualization and positive thinking."

EMBRACING THE BRIGHT SIDE

The pressures and challenges that you face at home, at school, and with your friends are nothing new. Many teens are going through the same things, though in different ways. You may not have all the beautiful clothes you fancy, and yet you still have enough food to eat each day. Be grateful for that. Another teen out there may have all that you desire, but they may not have the same brilliant and creative mind you have. When you start looking at the positive side of things and practicing gratitude for the things you have, no matter how little, you will start enjoying life more. Being cheerful and creating a good vibe around you attracts more of the things you like. Gratitude stops the negative thought pattern of what has hurt you before.

Practicing Patience as a Virtue

When you become patient with yourself, you will gradually be able to do the same with those around you. The people you hang around, and even strangers, will start liking you more. Patience involves embracing your flaws and making a resolve to do better next time after each failure. You probably love Disney movies and may have even been to the thrilling Disneyland before. But do you know the breathtaking history of the founder, Walt Disney? Well, is it not inspiring to hear that this famous creative genius was actually a slow learner in school? He was diagnosed with dyslexia, a condition that makes it difficult for one to speak properly or construct meaningful words and/or sentences. Disney was so focused on his imaginative, creative abilities that his school teachers actually became bothered by the description of his vivid mental pictures. However, by being patient with himself over the years, Disney honed his unique abilities and gradually became the superstar that he became known to be.

Benefits of a Happy Environment on Your Mind

Your desire to become who you want to be is attainable when you surround yourself with people who share a similar vision with you. When your peers like the things you do, and you love their presence too, the activities you engage in are more likely to promote your psychological development and general well-being. This makes you a happier person, with improved chances of achieving your dreams. When you do this constantly, even at home with your family, your mind gradually begins to adapt to a more positive frame.

With a positive mindset, you can allow your thoughts to enjoy the present experiences that you go through without the pains of the past or worries about tomorrow. This practice is known as mindfulness. You are less likely to feel overwhelmed or stressed when you focus on just the things you need to do at that time. This helps you to focus better on your school work, relationships, and overall performance. You will ultimately find it easier to visualize endless possibilities and solutions to problems, even in the midst of challenges.

Speaking and Thinking Positively

By consistently reaffirming your capabilities and speaking positively to yourself, you will begin to develop a nature that actually starts getting things done. When you do something remarkably well, other teens may feel jealous and speak ill about it just to get to you. The truth is they would actually love to be in your position, but they just can't, so they will say bad things to piss you off. In such cases, ignore the negative remarks and appreciate your strengths by rewarding yourself for a job well done. This will motivate you to do even better in the future and ultimately build more confidence.

As a teen, your mind is still developing and will believe the things you constantly tell it. That superstar you desire to be, speak it into being and watch your words come into being. Surrounding yourself with the people and environment that inspires you to be at your best will also work wonders in ultimately molding you to be who you want to be. Visualizing positive things and speaking them regularly will transform your life for the better and help you make the right choices in preparation for your adulthood.

CREATE YOUR DREAM REALITY

I'm sure you've heard it said that "dreams can be brought to reality by thinking, speaking, and acting on them" (Rosen, 2022). Well, this notion is true and holds even more during your teenage years. This is because this is the stage where your creative abilities are optimal since your brain is still developing and trying new things out. New ideas actually have limitless possibilities if you act upon them. This is why you need to start seriously considering those nagging thoughts that you usually have about trying out a new crazy thing just for the fun of it. Some of the world's most innovative inventions, like the airplane, are actually the brainchild of ideas that were initially thought to be crazy but later turned out to be historic.

Oprah Winfrey is a good example of how you can bring your dream realities into being. She used, and still uses, vision boards to help visualize the steps toward making her dreams a reality. Vision boards give clarity to the goals you set, such that you can actually visualize yourself achieving them. There are no strict rules to follow when creating vision boards. You can clearly map out each step the way you fancy based on the uniqueness of your dreams. Your life as a teenager is filled with various programmed schedules, including school and part-time work, as well as extracurricular activities like sports, entertainment, and dating. All this may make it difficult for you to concentrate on the important life choices to make. This is where the vision boards come in. Outline everything, from your work aspirations, personal extracurricular goals, and even timelines for each anticipated accomplishment, if you so wish. One good thing about vision boards is that there is no wrong way of making them.

Make the vision boards with due consideration to your feelings and emotions, and express them alongside each goal that you want to achieve. Visualizing your dream makes you walk in it in your mind, even before starting the actual physical steps. When you visualize yourself accomplishing something, especially at night before you sleep, the graphic mental picture gets deep into your subconscious realms and becomes a living part of you. You may often find yourself even dreaming about your vision while sleeping. Night dreams may actually add some creativity to the way you achieve your goals. Larry Page, the famous founder of Google, actually got the idea to start the company from a dream he had (Gillet, 2016).

BE BODY POSITIVE

During puberty, your body will certainly experience changes that are unique to you as an individual. Your body structure's peculiar features are beautiful the way they are. If you are slim, then you may probably excel in track events like sprinting. If you have a bigger body frame, you would likely do well in sporting events like the shot put, discus throw, weightlifting, and javelin. You will surely have a popular role model to look up to who has a similar body frame as yours and who does exceptionally well in their trade. The famous English footballer Peter Crouch was popular for his skinny and tall frame, which made him stand out and had people naturally falling in love with his style of play.

Embracing Your Unique Beauty

It is good for you to also realize that different societies usually have contrasting standards of what beauty, or the ideal body, is. As such, regardless of your body shape or skin color, it will always be considered beautiful in some circles. Better still, you could still define your own standard of beauty based on your appearance. Your body is still growing, so it will surely experience many changes as you grow. The key to adapting to these changes is to practice self-love for the way you look. You are awesome the way you are!

Regardless of your body shape and size, regular exercise will improve the way you look. Join a sports team of your choice and have fun with your colleagues while your body gets in shape. Give yourself enough time to sleep at night so that your body and mind can recover while you reignite your strength. Remember to have a healthy diet that includes plenty of vegetables, fruits, and unprocessed natural foods. These are good for keeping your still-growing body active, while meat and legumes will also help promote better growth of your body tissues. Drink plenty of water, too, to keep your body hydrated. When you make healthy choices for your body and take good mental and physical care of it, you boost your confidence.

The aim of this chapter was to help you realize the importance of bringing your dreams to reality by believing, visualizing, and acting toward them. Once a solid blueprint of your vision is imprinted on your mind, it becomes a matter of time before you achieve your dreams. Work on your mind and body to embrace your uniqueness, and you can achieve just about anything you set out to achieve. Also, get some tips on how you can attain emotional intelligence in the next chapter.

10

BE THE BOSS OF YOUR BRAIN

> *Being called weird is like being called a limited edition.*
> *Meaning you're something people don't see that often.*
> *Remember that.*

— ANDY BIERSACK

Emotional regulation and stress management are important aspects that you should learn as a teenager. Good management helps you to be a considerate, rational individual who is of good temperament. An emotion, by definition, is a strong feeling that emanates from one's mood, relationships, and circumstances. It can be distinguished from reasoning and knowledge and can be instinctive or intuitive. Emotional regulation involves the ability to control, strengthen, or use feelings, regardless of whether they are positive or negative.

Stress management is key for survival now and more so as you enter into adulthood. Stress management is defined as a collection of strategies that are meant to help individuals to deal with stress. The general idea behind dealing with stress is conditioning your mind and body to adapt to stressful situations. This helps you to live a healthier and more stable life. Your mind and body should acclimate to the fact that stress is a normal part of life, considering that we encounter challenging situations every now and then. This chapter was designed to address "emotional regulation and stress management," which represents the "E" on the B.R.A.V.E.S.T. framework.

WHAT IS EMOTIONAL INTELLIGENCE?

Emotional intelligence is simply the ability to feel, understand, control, assess, and use emotions so that you can relate and communicate with others. Communication that is done with the proper use of emotions is often effective and constructive. It is very important for you to learn to control emotions, but it is even more important for you to be able to effectively comprehend others' emotions.

Managing and understanding emotions involves recognizing and labeling emotions in oneself and in others. You should be able to understand what another person is trying to express. Therefore, emotional intelligence encompasses empathy, understanding, and relating to others' emotions (Cherry, 2022). It teaches you not to be self-centered but to be a team player in life, with the ability to positively contribute to livelihoods by effective use of emotions.

An emotionally intelligent person is able to communicate effectively. This means that you are able to bring across your thoughts, ideas, and feelings in the most effective of ways without erupting negative emotions in others. Emotional intelligence reflects good conflict-resolution skills. This means that you are able to calm the negative emotions in yourself and others while cultivating positive emotions and reaching common ground.

Emotionally intelligent people are able to build good social relationships and can better navigate social interactions. During your teen years, managing your emotions can be more difficult, especially with the various hormonal changes. You may have to work very hard to regulate your emotions. For you to cultivate emotional intelligence, strive for more self-awareness.

Emotional intelligence can be categorized into personal skills and interpersonal skills. Let's look at these two categories in more depth.

Personal Skills

There are three personal competencies that add up to emotional intelligence, and these are

- **Self-awareness:** This can be broken down into three areas, which are emotional awareness, self-confidence, and good self-assessment. Self-awareness is the ability to comprehend your own emotions as they come through. You should view emotions as either

appropriate or inappropriate, not as positive or
negative. When you practice effective self-awareness,
you build self-confidence and self-esteem.

- **Self-regulation:** This has to do with the ability to be
trustworthy, conscientious, adaptable, and innovative,
in addition to practicing self-control. Once you are
aware of your emotions, the next thing is to learn to
manage them well. This means that you should be able
to regulate and manage the emotions that you feel at
any given time.

- **Motivation:** This refers to the personal drive and desire
to achieve and improve. It includes a commitment to
your goals, readiness to act, and perseverance in
seeking opportunities. However, whatever you
motivate yourself on should be within reasonable
reach; otherwise, you might get frustrated. If you
cannot do something, be open and honest to yourself
and others about it.

Social or Interpersonal Skills

Interpersonal skills have a lot to do with how you interact with
others and with the environment. These skills help you to
formulate good relationships and understand others. The two
major aspects of interpersonal skills are

- **Empathy:** An empathic person is one who is aware of
how other people feel. They are able to perceive things
from the point of view of others. You are better able to
understand the situations of others and to help them

develop when you are empathetic. Empathy helps you to be an individual with a service orientation, aligning yourself to be of help to others. To cultivate empathy, learn to be a good listener.

- **Social skills:** Many of the social skills that you require to achieve emotional intelligence are rooted in self-esteem and confidence. A person with good social skills is easy to talk to because they are trustworthy and have good listening attributes. When you are able to master good social skills, you appear charismatic and, therefore, attract people to you.

Emotional intelligence is a vital aspect of your development. It improves your etiquette in emotional expression and has a very critical role in your personal growth and overall happiness. Emotional intelligence is a skill that is learned over time, so you don't need to be so hard on yourself. Therefore, you should dedicate yourself to investing the time and effort to master the skills that add up to emotional intelligence.

TAMING THE EMOTIONAL ROLLER COASTER

Teenage years are an emotional roller coaster for most people because as hormones flare, emotions may also go wild. You may even find yourself getting into trouble for things that you wouldn't have done if you had kept your emotions in check. There are several ways through which you can tame your emotions, and these include the following:

- **Practice self-awareness by identifying and reflecting on your emotions:** The best way to manage your emotions is to know them and reflect on them. To gain more insight into your emotional behavior, you can seek feedback from trusted individuals. This helps you to know yourself better, and this becomes the foundation for emotionally regulating yourself (Stade, 2017).
- **Seek to understand others' emotions:** Teach yourself to actively listen and understand how other people feel.
- **Develop effective communication skills to express emotions and needs:** As you mature into an adult, you need to learn better ways to communicate your needs. It would be very inappropriate for you to throw tantrums or shout in order to communicate your emotions and needs. You should focus more on communicating effectively in appropriate ways and with respect. When emotions get out of hand, you should learn to regulate them using techniques like deep breathing or journaling until you feel better.
- **Cultivate emotional resilience by embracing setbacks as learning opportunities:** When you embrace setbacks, you develop emotional resilience. One good way to do this is to focus on developing a positive and optimistic mindset while avoiding the "blame game." In cases where things do not work out, be compassionate to yourself and extend kindness to others. Understanding this will help you to keep your emotions in check.

- **Practice problem-solving skills:** You can learn self-regulation in cases of conflict by continuously practicing self-reflection, as well as being mindful and patient. Problem-solving skills can be developed over time. Therefore, continue seeking opportunities to get acquainted with your emotions through therapy, workshops, and books.

THE ANGER BEAST

From time to time, we all feel angry. However, in some cases, you may find that you are almost always angry, even at the smallest things. In that case, you will need to learn anger management techniques because uncontrolled anger can be detrimental. You might want to hear this short story about bad temper:

Once, there was a little boy with a terrible temper. To help him, his father gave him a bag of nails and advised him that each time he lost his temper, he should drive a nail into the fence. On the first day, the little boy drove 37 nails into the fence. As the weeks went by, he learned to control his anger, and the number of nails he had to drive into the fence kept reducing. Eventually, there came a day when he did not have to drive any nails into the fence.

The father was happy, and he told the boy to pull out a single nail for each day that he managed to keep a good temper. After many days, the boy told his father that there were no more nails on the fence. The father commended his son for managing to control his temper but pointed out that there were many holes in the fence. He told the boy that if he said things out of anger, no matter how many times he would apologize, his words would have left a scar.

Dealing With the Anger Beast

Teenage years are the years that shape your adulthood. Learning to deal with anger during this stage is a great idea. Here are some tips to help you deal with the anger beast:

- **Recognize anger triggers and early warning signs:** Usually, there are triggers and warning signs that show that you are about to get angry. You may just feel grumpy and irritable. Anxiety, fear, or tiredness are some triggers that may eventually present as anger. When you find yourself susceptible to anger, you can try taking deep breaths or count slowly from one to ten to calm yourself down. The idea is to distract yourself from the anger triggers.
- **Express anger assertively and communicate needs calmly:** Finding the right words to express yourself when you are feeling angry can be difficult. Often, people regret the things they say out of anger. You should learn assertiveness in order to communicate your anger effectively. It is one thing to feel angry and another to express it. Try to be as calm as possible. Assertive communication skills when expressing anger will also add up to good conflict-resolution skills.
- **Seek healthy outlets for anger, such as journaling or art:** Journaling acts as a very good outlet for anger. Try

to jot down how you are feeling, together with the associated triggers. It is also good to engage in physical activity. After good physical activity, you will find that you feel more emotionally calm and relaxed. Alternatively, you can use relaxation techniques like meditation.

- Seek support from trusted adults or professionals for guidance: In some cases, anger can be excessive and eventually become unhealthy. Knowing when to seek help is good for you. Anger problems may reflect in your actions, that is, being aggressive and violent. If uncontrolled, anger can affect your relationships, your job, or your career. Consider talking to trusted adults or going for therapy to learn to control anger.

Emotional regulation and stress management are vital skills that you should develop during your teenage years. Learning these skills helps you to grow into a temperamental adult who is capable of building solid relationships and making sound decisions. Once you are able to master your emotions and control anger, you will definitely achieve emotional intelligence. The next chapter focuses on offering strategies to help you overcome stress. You sure need to learn about that, so dig in!

11

STRESS BUSTERS

One day you'll look back and realize that you worried too much about things that didn't really matter.

— ANONYMOUS

We all experience stress at some point in our lives, irrespective of age. Although stress can be beneficial in driving us to operate under pressure and endure, it is not always required. Therefore, we should work hard to be more immune to its effects. Stress can contribute to self-distraction, causing you to lose focus on your day-to-day tasks. It can also affect your physical health.

In this chapter, we will explore how you can deal with stress. It's also important to note that the chapter works hand-in-hand with the previous one, which explores the "E" part of the B.R.A.V.E.S.T. framework. To begin with, here is a short story to get you ready. Once upon a time, there was a mouse that was terrified. It was being pursued by a large cat. As the mouse ran as fast as it could, it noticed a large grandfather clock and decided to climb on top of it to sit down and rest. A little while later, the clock landed on one, Dong!" The mouse was so surprised that he rushed down the clock (Raising Children Network, n.d.). When confronted with some circumstances, you should be brave. You should have greater confidence and fearlessness to tackle life's challenges. This will keep you safe from foes and dangers (Raising Children Network, n.d.).

WHAT IS STRESS?

Stress is an emotional reaction to outside obstacles, demands, or occurrences. These could include approaching due dates, hard choices, or illnesses. When faced with these instances, your body will let you know if you are worried. For example, your heart and breathing rates may increase while muscles may stiffen. Life is full of stress, and it's not always negative. Stress can prepare you for action and provide the drive to complete tasks. Instant stress about an imminent assessment can inspire you to put in the effort required in studying and preparing. Knowing that you should be on the bus on time can help you get ready in the morning.

ZEN ZONE

A Zen zone is commonly known as a place that allows you to meditate and get away from the outside chaos. Discovering a location like that can be helpful in that it can enhance tension relief, in addition to rebalancing the mind, body, and soul. Zen zones are quiet, peaceful, and isolated places where no one can disturb you. It doesn't need to be an expensive place somewhere; your room could make a good Zen zone. There are several places you can choose from to create your own personal Zen zone. The little nearby bush, the backyard, or a spot by the riverside—the choice is yours.

How would you know that you need a Zen zone? Here are some stress indications that show that you are possibly stressed enough to require time off in a Zen zone:

- anxiety or mood fluctuations
- inability to concentrate or make decisions
- changes in sleep schedules, causing insomnia or excessive sleeping
- appetite loss or overeating
- tiredness
- physical signs such as stomach pain, migraines, or muscle tightness
- loss of interest in social events or friendships
- worry or uneasiness
- feeling restless or overwhelmed
- loss of enthusiasm
- prolonged emotional outbursts
- gaming addiction
- consumption of drugs

Strategies for Reducing Stress

It is critical to manage stress symptoms as soon as you notice them in order to maintain excellent mental and physical health and continue with your day. Here are some suggestions to help you reduce stress:

- **Be physically active:** Exercising can improve your physical health while also enhancing your mood and sense of accomplishment. The stress hormone called cortisol is eliminated by fitness, and this can aid in physical relaxation.
- **Eat healthy food:** You will feel strong, vibrant, attentive, and able to focus if you eat healthily.
- **Unwind and relax:** You could try taking a stroll, reading a book, taking a soothing bath, listening to music, or practicing breathing, muscular relaxation, or meditation activities. This works quite well if you do it before bed.
- **Rest well:** As a young adult, you may need about eight to 10 hours of sleep per night. Enough high-quality sleep can make you feel more focused, upbeat, and energized.
- **Refrain from coffee, liquor, and other substances:** Liquor and other drugs are usually used by some teenagers to deal with stress. Sadly, these substances can also worsen the symptoms of stress and cause other health, mental, and psychological issues.

- **Deep breathing:** You can consider engaging in breathing exercises. Deep breathing makes you feel calmer and more at ease.

- **Mindfulness:** Being mindful means giving the present moment your full attention. It involves allowing your anxieties and ideas to arise and leave without you passing any judgment. You'll generally feel calmer and less distracted when you practice mindfulness. You'll also be able to see things clearly and make wise decisions.

- **Seek help:** If you frequently feel stressed out and struggle to deal with daily tasks, you might benefit from seeking additional support. Talking to your doctor, visiting the school counselor or psychologist, speaking with a spiritual leader or elder, or speaking to a youth worker could help. You could also consider going to eHeadspace.

- **Limit screen time:** Making sure that screen time doesn't disrupt sleep is another aspect of maintaining the appropriate balance that keeps you healthy. Too much screen time strains your brain and tends to increase stress.

- **Relaxation techniques**: Engage in meditation techniques such as meditation, guided imagery, or progressive muscle relaxation. These strategies will assist you in calming down and refocusing so that you can tackle the challenges that are causing you to be stressed.

- **Social support:** Talking to your parents or a friend about what is stressing you out can give you some sense of relief and comfort. This could lessen the stress and help you navigate your way out of the problem.

NAVIGATING THE SHADOWS: DEPRESSION

As a teenager, you can be afflicted by depression, which is a severe mental health illness. Some statistics show that one in every five teens has signs of depression at some point during their childhood or adolescence (Raising Children Network, 2019). Depression can have negative long-term effects on your mental health and general quality of life if it is not addressed.

Signs of Depression in Teenagers

Depression is a psychological disorder that results in a constant sense of melancholy, helplessness, and unworthiness. It is a relentless, overpowering mood that goes beyond feeling low or sad and can interfere with your ability to go about your everyday activities. Here are some signs of depression that you should be on the lookout for:

- a constant sense of hopelessness, irritability, or loss of interest in previously enjoyed activities
- alterations in appetite and sleeping habits (such as lack of appetite, difficulty falling asleep, or oversleeping)
- a decrease in strength
- feelings of regret or inadequacy
- having trouble focusing or making judgments

- physical signs of illnesses without a documented medical cause (such as headaches, stomach aches, and muscle pain)
- isolation from family and close friends
- occasional thoughts of self-harm or suicide

Dealing With Depression

Depression is a common mental condition that can worsen if not treated immediately. Overcoming depression is often challenging, especially as a teenager going through puberty. Here are some strategies for overcoming depression:

- taking antidepressants
- visiting a family therapist
- receiving counseling
- joining support clubs
- meditation
- taking part in physical hobbies
- being around loved ones and avoiding isolation
- being kind to yourself
- following a healthy routine
- reciting daily affirmations and focusing on positive thoughts

MINDFUL MATTERS

Mindfulness is a deliberate way of paying full attention to the current situation rather than the past or future without criticism. The nonjudgmental mindset is critical because we tend to criticize our thoughts. Being conscious of our thoughts and learning to accept them can result in a profound shift in the way we see ourselves. As a teenager, mindfulness can be an excellent method for development and a coping skill in stressful situations. There are various mindful practices that you can do daily to help you with your demands. It's fine to begin practicing mindfulness by experimenting with several strategies to determine which ones work best for you. Different hobbies may also have varied benefits; for example, some may promote rest while others may promote awareness.

Here are some of the mindful activities that you can consider practicing:

- **Mindful walking:** Become one with your surroundings as you take a walk.
- **Gratitude practice:** Be grateful and proud of what you've accomplished so far.
- **Scan your body:** Examine your body for tightness and do some exercises to release the tension.
- **Be present:** Focus on the now and let go of any negative thoughts from the past, especially those that cause regret and anxiety.
- **Mindful eating:** Examine a bite of fruit or sweets, paying attention to color, texture, and scent.
- **Practice deep breathing:** Breathing exercises are a mindfulness technique that involves taking deep, calm breaths via the diaphragm. This promotes calmness.

- **Light a candle:** One method for meditation and mind freedom is to light a candle and watch it in a calm environment.
- **Journal writing:** Allow yourself to write about your daily life in a book. This can help you relieve tension and provide insight into making smart judgments.

Stress and depression share similar symptoms, such as difficulty sleeping, loss of appetite, headaches, and difficulty concentrating. It is nearly impossible not to encounter these types of experiences during your adolescent years, which is why taking the correct actions, such as deep breathing, journaling, meditating, and being kind to yourself, will help you. Depression is a long-term condition that can be tough to overcome, which is why you don't have to go through it alone. You can see a family therapist and join support groups. The next chapter will help you navigate your way through friendships and guide you in selecting the right crowd that will support you in your real-life experiences.

12

FINDING YOUR TRIBE

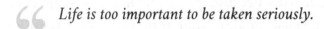 *Life is too important to be taken seriously.*

— OSCAR WILDE

Considering how important life is, especially at the stage that you are, you better live it with the right people around you. As you navigate the complex landscape of adolescence, it is natural to seek out like-minded teens who possess the same interests, values, and ideas as yours. Your tribe consists of those who understand you on a deeper level, thereby providing a sense of belonging and acceptance. They are the friends who make you feel seen and heard, the ones with whom you can be your authentic self. This chapter is going to explore the importance of friendships and strategies for resisting peer pressure. It will also equip you with conflict resolution skills, which is partly why it perfectly fits under the "S" part of the

B.R.A.V.E.S.T. framework, which talks about "social matters and empathy."

"Jerry and Jenny, two sailors, set out to prove the Earth was round by sailing around the world. They embarked on a voyage from Singapore, but as they approached the end, the sunset was in the wrong direction. Confused and alarmed, they sailed on for days, weeks, and years, but never found land or completed their journey. They realized they had been sailing on a flat earth, trapped in an endless ocean, forever lost (Roberts, 2021)." Jerry and Jenny's journey emphasizes the importance of actively seeking out like-minded individuals to form your tribe. Jerry and Jenny were on a mission to prove a theory, but they were ultimately unsuccessful because they didn't have the support or guidance they needed. Finding your tribe provides a sense of direction, support, and acceptance, helping you navigate life's challenges and stay true to yourself. They become friends who understand and appreciate your authentic self, creating a community that will lead to personal growth and fulfillment.

FINDING YOUR BFFS

Building friendships is an important part of teenage life. It is a chance to connect with others, form bonds, and create a network of support. Making friends can be a rewarding experience that contributes to your overall well-being and happiness. To help you navigate the process, here are some tips you should consider:

- **Be yourself:** One of the most crucial aspects of making friends is being true to yourself. Authenticity is attractive and will help you attract friends who will understand you. Trying to be a different person might lead to exhaustion and dissatisfaction in the long run. Embrace your unique qualities and let your true personality shine.

- **Communicate openly:** Honest and open communication is the foundation of any strong friendship. You should honestly express your thoughts, feelings, and expectations to your friends and encourage them to do the same. This creates a level of trust and understanding that is essential for building deep connections.

- **Set boundaries:** It is essential to establish personal boundaries while you respect those of others. You should clearly define what you are comfortable with and communicate it to your friends. This could include things like personal space, privacy, or limits on certain activities.

- **Choose quality over quantity:** Instead of focusing on having too many friends, aim at developing a few genuine and meaningful friendships. Quality friends aid support and companionship, and you are less likely to have avoidable disagreements.

- **Accept differences:** Embracing diversity and appreciating the unique qualities that each friend brings to the relationship is of paramount importance. Everyone has their interests, backgrounds, and perspectives. Instead of judging or trying to change others, celebrating the differences and learning from each other will curb the chances of disagreements.

- **Practice active listening:** You should show genuine interest in your friends by actively listening to them. Consider giving them your undivided attention and showing empathy and understanding, especially during their hard times. You should also avoid interrupting or jumping to conclusions. If you listen attentively, you show that you value their thoughts and feelings. Active listening also allows you to learn more about each other and deepen your connection.
- **Offer support:** A good friendship is built on mutual support. It is vital that you celebrate success together and help each other in tough times.
- **Balance give and take:** Friendships are a two-way street, and it is essential to find a balance between giving and receiving support. Be willing to help your friends when they need it, whether it is giving advice or simply being there for them. At the same time, be open to accepting support from your friends when you need it. Allow them to be there for you and let them contribute to the friendship as well. If you maintain a healthy balance of give and take, the friendship remains equitable and mutually beneficial.
- **Avoid toxic friendships:** It is crucial to recognize and distance yourself from toxic friendships. Toxic friendships are characterized by negativity, manipulation, or a lack of respect. If you find yourself

in a toxic friendship, consider stepping away and prioritizing your well-being.

- **Embrace new connections:** You should be open to meeting new people and expanding your social network. This is done by stepping out of your comfort zone and joining clubs, participating in activities, or attending events that align with your interests. This opens up opportunities to meet like-minded individuals and form new friendships. You should approach new connections with an open mind and a willingness to learn from others.

RISE ABOVE THE CROWD

Peer pressure could be even more prevalent and possibly dangerous during your teenage years. It is that feeling of being influenced by your friends to do something that you might not be comfortable with. This section highlights some of the methods for handling it and being true to yourself.

- **Educate yourself:** It is vital to educate yourself about the risks and consequences that are associated with peer pressure. Once you are aware of the risks, you become empowered to make informed decisions that align with your values and well-being.
- **Trust your instincts:** Trusting your instincts is another essential aspect of handling peer pressure. Your inner voice and personal values serve as effective guides in making choices. Listen to that little voice inside you

that tells you what feels right and wrong. If you think that the decision you are about to make does not align with your values, honor your instincts.

- **Surround yourself with positive influences:** Identify individuals who have goals and ideas that align with yours. Positive friendships provide a strong support system that encourages you to make healthy choices.

- **Learn to say "No":** If you can say "no," you will be in a better position to handle peer pressure. It is not wrong to decline an invitation or to express your preferences and choices. If you set limits, it shows that you are committed to your goals, and this helps you to curb the negative impacts of peer pressure.

- **Seek supportive adults:** When faced with challenging situations, seeking the guidance and support of trusted adults can be immensely helpful. Trusted adults can include parents, teachers, counselors, or mentors who can offer advice and different perspectives. They can provide reassurance and help you navigate through difficult decisions.

- **Focus on your goals:** Focusing on your goals can assist you in resisting peer pressure. If you keep your aspirations and priorities clear, you can make choices that align with your long-term vision. Whether it is academic success, personal growth, or pursuing a passion, staying focused on your goals can provide the motivation and determination that you need to resist negative influences.

- **Practice assertiveness and develop self-confidence:** Confidently expressing your opinions and making your own choices is key when handling peer pressure. Remember, it is normal to have differing viewpoints from those of your friends. You should respectfully communicate your thoughts and preferences, asserting your independence and individuality. You should also cultivate a strong sense of self-worth and identity. When you believe in yourself and your values, it becomes easier to resist the influence of others.

- **Seek alternative activities:** You should engage in hobbies, sports, or extracurricular activities that bring you joy and fulfillment. If you immerse yourself in positive and fulfilling activities, you naturally gravitate toward friends who share your interests and values.

- **Develop a support network and trustworthy friends:** Building a support network of friends who share your values is crucial in handling peer pressure. You need to surround yourself with individuals who respect and support your choices. True friends will celebrate and appreciate you for who you are, providing a safe and supportive environment.

SETTLE DIFFERENCES LIKE A PRO

Conflicts exist in our daily lives, and being able to resolve them constructively and respectfully requires special skills and strategies that you can learn over time. Let's explore some valuable conflict resolution techniques that are specifically designed for you in this section.

- **Active listening and understanding:** One crucial aspect of conflict resolution is active listening. It involves paying attention to the other person and seeking to understand their perspective. When engaging in a conflict, take the time to listen attentively without interrupting or making assumptions. Actively listening demonstrates that you respect and want to create a conducive environment for finding common ground.
- **Express your feelings and needs clearly:** Using "I" statements is an excellent way to express your feelings and needs without sounding accusatory. Instead of saying, "You never listen to me," try saying, "I feel frustrated when I don't feel heard." This approach allows you to communicate your emotions and needs while maintaining an open and constructive dialogue.
- **Finding common ground and solutions:** During conflicts, you should shift your focus from blame to finding common ground and seeking solutions. Instead of dwelling on who is right or wrong, explore ways to address everyone's needs. If you adopt a cooperative mindset, you can work together to find win-win solutions that benefit everyone involved.
- **Practicing empathy and considering impact:** Empathy plays a crucial role in conflict resolution. Put yourself in the other person's shoes and try to understand their feelings and perspectives. Recognize that your actions can have a negative impact on others, and consider how your words and behaviors might be affecting them. This empathy allows for greater

understanding and paves the way for more effective communication.

- **Respecting communication and avoiding personal attacks:** Respectful communication is vital during conflicts. You need to avoid resorting to personal attacks or derogatory language that can escalate tensions. Instead, focus on the issue at hand and express your thoughts and concerns in a respectful manner. Remember, the goal is to find a resolution, not to win an argument.

- **Taking responsibility and apologizing:** Taking responsibility for your actions is a sign of maturity and a crucial step in conflict resolution. If you realize that you have made a mistake or hurt someone, show willingness to apologize. Apologizing shows humility and a willingness to repair the relationship.

- **Seeking mediation or guidance:** In some cases, conflicts may require outside assistance. If you find it challenging to resolve a conflict on your own, consider seeking mediation or involving a trusted adult for guidance. Mediators can help facilitate communication and guide the parties involved toward a resolution. Trusted adults, such as parents, teachers, or mentors, can offer valuable insights and support during difficult situations.

- **Practicing patience and allowing emotions to calm down:** Conflicts can evoke strong emotions, and it is of significant importance that you give yourself time to calm down. Learn to avoid making hasty decisions or saying things you might regret later. Take a step back, and give yourself and others space to process their emotions so that you resume the conversation when everyone is calmer.

- **Seeking compromise and finding creative solutions:** Conflict resolution often involves finding compromises that satisfy everyone's needs to some extent. You should be open to exploring different options and brainstorming creative solutions together.
- **Reflection and growth:** After a conflict is resolved, take the opportunity to reflect on the experience. Consider what you have learned from the conflict and how it can contribute to your personal growth. Reflecting on conflicts helps to build self-awareness and equips you with valuable insights for future situations.
- **Fostering respect, understanding, and cooperation:** Conflict resolution is not just about resolving individual differences but fostering a culture of respect, understanding, and cooperation in all relationships. When you practice these conflict resolution skills consistently, you contribute to creating a positive and harmonious environment where conflicts are resolved constructively.

This chapter unleashed the importance of friendships and valuable strategies for developing and sustaining genuine connections. It is key that you resist peer pressure by trusting your instincts, setting clear boundaries, and surrounding yourself with positive influence. Additionally, you can develop essential conflict resolution skills by active listening, using "I" statements, and seeking win-win solutions. If you embrace these concepts, you can navigate social situations with confidence and build healthy relationships that contribute to your overall well-being. The next chapter will delve deeper into how you can develop positive family relationships.

13

FAMILY FEATS

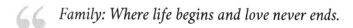 *Family: Where life begins and love never ends.*

— ANONYMOUS

Isn't this quote so true? Family is where it all begins, and no matter what happens, love is always there, even in the midst of chaos. It's apparent that not every family is picture-perfect or traditional, but that does not mean that you cannot create a supportive and nurturing environment where your emotional and psychological well-being can grow. If you do not have a traditional family, this chapter will assist you with creating strategies that empower you to thrive and cultivate a sense of happiness. It also handles the social aspects of your teenage life, so it also falls under the "S" of the B.R.A.V.E.S.T. framework.

To begin with, let's talk about the Wacky family who went camping in Quirksville. They were known for being funny and doing silly things. Mr. Wacky was clumsy, and he made everyone laugh while setting up the tent. Mrs. Wacky told jokes with a rubber chicken while the kids, Benny and Bella, organized fun games for everyone to play. Even the serious campers couldn't help but laugh and have a good time. The Wacky family showed everyone that it's vital to enjoy life and relax a bit. People loved the funny camping adventures of the Wacky family, and it reminded them to embrace their own unique and silly sides. This story teaches us that humor and light-heartedness are crucial in strengthening family bonds and relationships. It shows that sharing laughter and embracing each other's quirks can create a positive and joyful atmosphere within a family setup. It highlights the importance of finding moments of fun and laughter together, enhancing a deeper connection, and creating lasting memories (McCabe, 2017).

FAMILY IS WHERE IT'S AT

The role of the family is irreplaceable and invaluable. It serves as a foundation of support, love, and guidance during this crucial stage of your life. Let's take a closer look at why family or a similar company holds such significance for you. It offers

- **Emotional support and a sense of belonging**: Family is there to provide a shoulder to lean on, offering comfort, understanding, and encouragement during challenging times. Your family members may listen to you without judgment, offer words of wisdom, and provide a safe space for you to express your feelings. Additionally, a family is a place where you can feel accepted and valued and experience a true sense of belonging.

- **Unconditional love, stability, and security:** Family members are more likely to love you unconditionally, embracing you for who you are, regardless of your flaws. This unwavering love becomes a source of strength and confidence as you navigate the ups and downs of adolescence. Knowing that you are loved and accepted by your family creates a secure foundation from which you can explore your own identity and relationships with others. Family offers a stable and secure environment for you to grow, explore, and flourish.

- **Shared values and traditions:** Most families instill values and traditions that shape your beliefs, behaviors, and character. These shared experiences create lasting memories and a sense of belonging. Family rituals, such as holiday traditions or weekly family dinners, further enhance a sense of connection.

- **Lifelong relationships, guidance, and mentorship:** The bonds that are formed within the family pave the way to lifelong connections and relationships. Siblings, parents, and extended family members become a support system that you can rely on throughout your life. The family members also serve as guides and mentors, offering valuable advice in all aspects of life.

- **Emotional development and identity formation:** In a family setup, you can learn to navigate through your emotions, develop empathy, and build emotional intelligence. Family relationships can provide a safe space to express and understand your emotions, contributing to your overall growth and resilience. Family plays a significant role in shaping your sense of self and identity.
- **Cultural heritage:** Family preserves and passes down cultural traditions, customs, and values, connecting you to your roots and supporting a sense of pride in your cultural heritage. Through cultural celebrations, language, and traditions, you can learn about your family's history and the importance of your cultural identity.
- **Learning from experiences:** Family members share experiences, wisdom, and life lessons that offer valuable insights. They provide guidance based on their own journeys, empowering you to make informed choices and learn from successes and setbacks.
- **Building social skills:** Family interactions enhance effective communication, conflict resolution, and cooperation.

PLAYING YOUR PART FOR A HARMONIOUS HOME

Fostering family harmony is an important aspect of creating a loving and supportive home environment. When family members feel connected, understood, and valued, it strengthens the bonds that hold them together. Interestingly, you have a role to play in developing such a haven. Let's see how you can achieve that.

- **Practice open communication and show appreciation:** You should promote open dialogue within the family, allowing members to freely express their thoughts, feelings, and concerns. This supports understanding, resolves conflicts, and strengthens family connections. Additionally, showing appreciation for each family member's efforts and contributions cultivates a positive and supportive atmosphere, as it validates their roles within the family.
- **Promote shared responsibility in household chores:** Train yourself to take part in household chores, as this cultivates a sense of teamwork and shared ownership.
- **Practice empathy and solve conflicts peacefully:** Resolving conflicts peacefully and constructively through open discussions, active listening, and finding mutually agreeable solutions promotes harmony, in addition to strengthening relationships.
- **Set boundaries and participate in family activities:** You should establish and respect boundaries within the family so that you honor personal space and individuality. This promotes healthy communication, minimizes misunderstandings, and fosters a balanced and harmonious environment. Additionally, engaging in family activities and quality time together strengthens the familial bond.
- **Support your siblings and show respect:** Encouraging your siblings to uplift and assist one another provides a

sense of camaraderie and mutual support within the family unit. Furthermore, consider showing kindness, patience, and respect to every family member to introduce an atmosphere of love and acceptance.

- **Be accountable and foster a positive atmosphere**: Holding oneself accountable for mistakes and offering sincere apologies when needed nurtures trust and understanding among family members. Being accountable teaches humility and forgiveness and demonstrates a commitment to maintaining healthy relationships.

- **Express love, care, and support regularly:** You need to verbalize affection, show care, and provide support because these are important for nurturing family relationships.

REDEFINING THE FAMILY: THRIVING WITHOUT TRADITIONAL TIES

Dealing with a dysfunctional family can be really tough, and it can take a toll on your emotional well-being. However, there are strategies that can help you navigate through such challenging situations, and we will discuss some of these in this section.

- **Seek support:** Check out local organizations or services that offer support for individuals dealing with dysfunctional family dynamics. These resources can include support groups, workshops, or counseling services specifically tailored to address family challenges. Connecting with these resources can provide additional guidance, insights, and a sense of belonging.

- **Create your chosen family:** Your biological family may not always be the source of the comfort and support you need. That's why it's important to build a chosen family of friends and loved ones who can provide the understanding and encouragement that you deserve.
- **Develop resilience:** Dealing with a dysfunctional family can be emotionally draining, but remember that you have inner strength. Focus on personal growth and finding ways to bounce back from challenges.
- **Find positive role models:** You should look for positive role models who can inspire you and show you what healthy relationships look like. Books, movies, or even real-life figures in your community could assume such roles in your life, whether knowingly or otherwise. Seeing examples of healthy dynamics can give you hope and guide you in creating your own positive relationships.
- **Seek therapy or counseling:** Therapists or counselors can provide guidance, support, and a safe space to explore your emotions and experiences.
- **Pursue healthy relationships:** You have to surround yourself with positive influences and supportive friends. Seek out relationships that uplift and encourage you. Being around people who genuinely care about your well-being and who bring positivity into your life can make a significant difference.

- **Educate yourself:** Take the initiative to learn about healthy relationships and effective coping strategies. Consider educating yourself through books, articles, or online resources that provide insights into navigating dysfunctional family dynamics. This will equip and prepare you to handle the challenges that come your way.

- **Practice boundary setting and focus on personal goals:** You need to clearly express your needs and limitations to your family members, allowing you to assert your personal space and define what is acceptable and what is not. Directing your attention toward your personal goals and aspirations helps you find fulfillment and purpose beyond the dynamics of your family environment.

- **Remember, you are not alone:** Remember, you are not alone in this journey. You should seek support from individuals who have faced similar challenges, as they can provide understanding, guidance, and a sense of validation to help you navigate through your experiences. Together, you can find strength and resilience to create a healthier and happier path going forward.

The chapter emphasized the importance of family relationships, offered strategies for a happy home, and addressed how you can thrive in dysfunctional or non-traditional family settings. Aspects such as open communication, appreciation, empathy, and conflict resolution were clearly highlighted. Strategies for thriving in non-traditional family settings include seeking support, creating a chosen family, and developing resilience. The goal is to ensure that you thrive, irrespective of the circumstances surrounding your life. Let us proceed to the next chapter, which explains the tools that you can use on social media.

14

SOCIAL MEDIA SAVVY

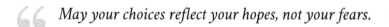 *May your choices reflect your hopes, not your fears.*

— NELSON MANDELA

Once upon a time, there was a woman who kept a mongoose as a pet. The mongoose was extremely trust-worthy. The woman left her infant with the pet while she went shopping. A large snake then entered their home and was killed by the mongoose after a long and violent struggle. The mongoose was lying at the entrance when the woman returned. She spotted its bloody mouth. Out of the heist, the woman thought that the mongoose had killed her child. The woman killed the mongoose by tossing the water jug at it in a fit of rage. She was overcome with regret when she saw a big cobra lying dead while her child was cheerfully playing. Prior to making any decisions, always give them careful thought because you never know how they may affect you or those around you (English for Students, n.d.). In this chapter, we will explore how you can use social media properly, along with how your online decisions affect you and those around you. It is based on the "S" section of the B.R.A.V.E.S.T. framework.

Today, I'm sure we all find it difficult to live without our phones, computers, and other electronics that enable us to connect to the internet. That's how most of us communicate with our loved ones, complete assignments, do grocery shopping, and stay up to date with the latest news. While the internet can be quite helpful in many things, it can also be a tool for wasting time and may even compromise your safety.

CYBER CITIZENSHIP

Cyber citizenship is the act of using the web in a way that is morally upright, safe, and ethical. You have a duty to use the internet in a safe, wise, and caring way as a cyber citizen of a dynamically linked society. The internet is a place where you should find balance in terms of opportunities and threats. Positive internet usage encourages others to act ethically and responsibly. Other teenagers can benefit from a digital world where there is a sense of collective optimism. Here are some ways in which you can practice cyber citizenship:

- **Positive posts:** Acknowledge the emotions and sentiments of others before posting. Focus on meaningful conversations rather than making disrespectful or disparaging remarks. Spend some time gathering yourself, then give compliments rather than criticism. To develop trust and support, concentrate on constructive discussion and encouraging feedback.

- **Respect personal privacy:** Doxxing is a misdemeanor; thus, it is not acceptable to disclose someone else's private details online without that person's consent (MLC, n.d.). Doxxing is a negative behavior since it involves disseminating personal information with the intent to harass, threaten, or incite violence.

- **Don't be a thief:** Respect others' creator ownership rights online by not taking or destroying their digital creations, identities, or property. Prior to using material that isn't yours, always get permission, and after getting it, be sure to give credit.

- **Share resources:** Before passing along any information that you find online that you think others in your network might find beneficial, make sure it's accurate.

- **Become a role model:** A better online environment always starts with you. Other people who look up to you may copy your good online etiquette.

- **Practice empathy:** Imagine how you would like to be treated. Everyone could use a little more optimism, so be respectful and kind to those who are in your online social circle.

- **Avoid cyberbullying:** Refrain from mocking other people or making threats. Always aim to show some kindness because you may never know what someone is going through. Many times, cyberbullying may lead to suicide, so your kind gesture might just save a life.

- **Fight back against negativity:** If you see someone being harassed or tormented online, speak out for them by reporting the offensive content to the hosting sites. The same applies to online material that could potentially be detrimental to other people. This includes violent, risky, or self-harming material, as well as racist comments and inaccurate information. Most websites give you the option to flag posts that are offensive, false, or racially insensitive. You can make the internet a better place for everyone just by reporting harmful information.

- **Don't publicly humiliate others:** Have you ever shared a cruel comment to belittle someone or uploaded a video of "bad behavior?" Due to the quick sharing and commenting capabilities of social media, it is now simpler than ever for teenagers to track down and "punish" specific users for actions that are deemed offensive or inappropriate. In many of these situations, the defendant is subjected to abusive comments and death threats, in addition to possibly having his or her confidential details made public. This may result in humiliation and harassment, which is why it is not advised to take matters into your own hands but rather report the issue to avoid any further damage.

UNPLUG AND RECHARGE

Maintaining relationships with the people in our lives through social media may be pleasant. However, the more time you spend online, the less time you're likely to spend with your real-world friends and family or even engage in your interests. You won't even have enough time to pay attention to your job or schoolwork. The best course of action is to develop healthy internet habits that balance online time with offline interaction and constructive hobbies. Spending too much time on social media can be harmful to your mental and physical well-being. This is why it is important for you to reset and take a break from social media. Here is how you can balance social media and the real world:

- **Take baby steps:** You can start by setting a goal to use social media for an hour less every week, which will free up one hour each week for activities that are excellent for your physical and mental health.
- **Exercise:** Exercising regularly and avoiding screens can be done by jogging, swimming, walking, or even yoga.
- **Explore your artistic side:** Investigate your options for self-expression, such as journaling, poem writing, drawing, learning how to play the guitar, and painting.
- **Disable push notifications:** Notifications tempt you to open apps, thereby attracting you to an online environment. Switching them off can help you avoid using apps.
- **Delete social media apps:** If you don't want to completely remove apps, you can archive them. Alternatively, you can move them from your primary home screen to limit the amount of time you spend on social media.
- **Establish "No Phone Zones":** For instance, refrain from checking your mobile device in bed at night or first thing in the morning. Also, avoid using your phone at the dinner table.

- **Use an app tracker:** Monitor how much time you spend on the internet by using an app tracker. Many applications come with timers that you may use to keep track of how much time you spend on them. Such trackers can notify you when it's time to close the app.
- **Prioritize face-to-face connections:** Doing this is a positive move whenever you decide to converse with friends or family in person rather than browsing through social media.

Establishing a healthy balance in the way you use social media can enable you to look after your mental well-being and develop longer-lasting, more constructive social networking habits. You will create good networking connections with other users, whether business-wise or in friendship, by being a cybercitizen. In the following chapter, we'll go into greater detail on determining your life's purpose, setting and achieving goals, and navigating the social pressures that influence your choices.

15

FUTURE FRONTIERS

 Dream higher than the sky and deeper than the ocean.

— ANONYMOUS

Being distinct is what sets you apart and makes you extraordinary. You might enjoy this little animal story. Once upon a time, birds were living happily in their nests on a mango tree in a jungle. They prepared for the rainy season by repairing their nests and collecting food. When the rains came, a monkey sought shelter but couldn't fit in the birds' nests. One bird sympathized with the monkey, who, instead of appreciating the advice that it was being given, was so angry. The monkey destroyed the bird's nest, leaving the birds without shelter. The realization that there are some people who don't appreciate good advice can be quite funny. The bird was only trying to help, after all. Hopefully, you choose not to disregard good advice because you certainly need it as you project into the future. By the time you get to the end of this chapter, you will have attained a basic understanding of how to explore your career options. You will also learn how to set SMART goals as well as handle the pressure and expectations that others impose on you. Please note that this chapter handles the final part of the B.R.A.V.E.S.T. framework, which is "tomorrow and times to come," represented by "T."

DISCOVERING YOUR PASSIONS: EXPLORING CAREER OPTIONS

Discovering your passions is an ongoing journey of self-exploration and self-discovery, as it involves diving deep into your interests, curiosities, and talents to uncover what truly ignites your soul. It also brings you a sense of purpose and fulfillment. Let's go through some suggestions on how you can discover your passions.

- **Know your interests:** Engage in and learn about things that truly capture your interest and curiosity. This involves delving into hobbies, topics, or experiences that fascinate and inspire you. By exploring these captivating activities, you can get to discover new passions, expand your knowledge, and find joy in the process. You can ask yourself self-driven questions like, "What kind of activities do I enjoy doing?" or "What topics do I like to learn about?" Honest answers to such questions will connect you to the things that you are passionate about.

- **Embark on research on different professions:** Be sure to research various professions and industries. This will help you to gain insights into the different career options that are available and also the industries they belong to. Understanding various professions and industries can help you make informed choices about career paths.
- **Seek mentorship and gain practical experience:** Seeking mentorship as a teenager can be an intimidating task, but it's a crucial step in preparing for your future. Actively reach out to experienced individuals in your field of interest or desired industry who can offer you valuable guidance and insights. Finding a mentor can be done through networking events, professional organizations, online communities, or even through personal connections. Be sure to pursue internships, part-time jobs, or volunteer opportunities. With these, you open doors to gaining hands-on experience in your field of interest. You can even explore different areas to discover your strengths and preferences. This experience offers you the chance to work on real projects, collaborate with professionals, and learn from their practical expertise.
- **Attend career fairs and take career assessments:** Career fairs are events where employers and organizations from different industries come together to showcase their work, discuss potential job openings, and provide information about their respective fields. Attending career fairs as a teenager offers you a valuable opportunity to explore diverse career options,

all in one place. Career assessments are designed to help you gain insights into your strengths, interests, values, and other characteristics that play a significant role in determining career satisfaction and success. These assessments typically involve questionnaires or exercises that provide you with a better understanding with regard to your unique traits and preferences.

- **Explore educational pathways, network with professionals, and shadow professionals:** Researching colleges and universities allows you to gather information about their academic programs, faculty, overall reputation, and campus culture. It is important to consider factors such as location, available resources, financial aid options, and the specific courses or majors offered. Remember to build connections and establish relationships with individuals who are already in your desired industry. This helps you to access firsthand insights into the day-to-day realities of the industry that you want to pursue.

- **Engage in informational interviews, experiment with side projects, and stay updated on industry trends:** Conducting interviews with professionals in your industry is key as it equips you with a deeper understanding of a specific profession. Actively spend more of your time in creative and entrepreneurial endeavors that are outside your main activities, such as work or education. This further assists you in exploring your passions and interests. Side projects are fantastic opportunities to delve into activities that bring you joy and allow you to express your creativity. Seek and remain informed about the latest developments, advancements, and shifts happening within your industry or field of interest. Such knowledge keeps you updated on the requirements that are associated with the industry that you fancy.

MAPPING YOUR PATH: SMART GOAL SETTING FOR FUTURE SUCCESS

Mastering the concept of setting goals is one of the aspects that orient you toward being successful in life. Setting relevant goals enables you to define the steps that are necessary to progress toward your desired destination. It also helps you to chart a course that aligns with your values, passions, and aspirations so that you can take intentional actions to navigate your way forward. In this section, we will look at how you can best create goals that can form the foundation of anything that you desire to do in life.

Create Goals Based on the SMART Criteria

As mentioned previously, SMART is simply an acronym that stands for Specific, Measurable, Achievable, Relevant, and Time-Bound. Let's explore SMART goals in more depth:

- **Specific:** You should define the specific details around your goals. For example, mention exactly what you want to do. Set clear objectives that state what you want to accomplish. For example, instead of saying, "I want to improve my coding skills," why not specify, "I want

to learn JavaScript and be able to build a functional
website."

- **Measurable:** You should identify concrete metrics or
  indicators that will help you track your progress and
  determine if you have achieved your goal. This could
  involve quantifiable measures like "increase revenue by
  20%" or "lose 10 pounds in three months." This way,
  you can clearly notice if you are making progress
  or not.
- **Achievable:** Normalize setting realistic goals that you
  can attain based on your current capabilities, available
  resources, and the time that you are willing to invest.
  Setting up goals that you are less likely to achieve will
  only frustrate you, and this may negatively affect your
  self-esteem.
- **Relevant:** A relevant goal is one that aligns with your
  overall objectives, values, and aspirations. Such goals
  are more likely to have significance and meaning to you
  because they directly contribute to your long-term
  vision. As a result, they are a direct motivation for you
  to achieve your goals.
- **Time-Bound:** Be sure to specify a timeline or deadline
  for achieving your goal. This helps create a sense of
  urgency and allows you to stay accountable. For
  instance, "I want to complete the first draft of my novel
  within six months" or "I will learn a new language
  fluently in one year." These goals have clear timelines
  that can also help you to assess your progress.

Break Your Goals Into Smaller Steps

Be sure to break down your goals into smaller, actionable steps that are manageable. This provides a clear roadmap and helps you to stay focused. For example, if your goal is to start a business, actionable steps could include "developing a business plan," "registering the business," and "launching a marketing campaign." By clearly defining your goal with specific details and outcomes, you enhance your motivation and ability to work toward achieving it.

Seek Support

Reach out to individuals who have knowledge, experience, and insights to help you navigate through challenges. This will also enhance your ability to make informed decisions. Peers who are also pursuing similar goals to yours can offer a unique perspective and a sense of camaraderie. They can provide emotional support, share resources and knowledge, as well as act as accountability partners.

It is important that you approach individuals with respect and genuine curiosity. Ensure that you have a clear understanding of your goals and what you aspire to achieve from the relationship. When you are talking to people who support you, actively listen to their insights, ask thoughtful questions, and be receptive to feedback and advice.

Regularly Evaluate, Adjust, and Celebrate Milestones

Periodically assess your progress, and make necessary adjustments. Acknowledging and celebrating the milestones that you achieved along the way is also of paramount importance, as it gives you a sense of reward while motivating you to continue making progress.

Stay Motivated, Stay Focused, and Track Progress

Cultivate a positive mindset, find inspiration, and remind yourself of the reasons why you set up the goals in the first place. Remember, staying focused and staying motivated go hand in hand. Motivation provides the drive, while focus ensures that your efforts are directed toward the right activities.

Remember to keep a record of how far you've come, identify patterns, and make informed adjustments to your strategies. Doing this provides a historical reference that allows you to appreciate the overall progress you've made.

HANDLING THE HEAT: MANAGING PRESSURE AND EXPECTATIONS

Effective management and coping with situations or conditions where there is intense pressure, stress, or conflict is a key aspect of handling internal pressure. Here are some tips that are worth noting:

- **Define your path and communicate your goals:** Be sure to step away from societal expectations or pressures. Rather, focus on what truly resonates with you. When you prioritize your dreams and aspirations, you take ownership of your life and make choices that align with your truest self.
- **Be around positive influences:** Being with individuals who have faith in your vision and those who are prepared to provide support throughout your journey is crucial. Don't be afraid to ask for feedback and ideas from others because engaging in conversations and actively listening to different perspectives can lead to valuable insights and partnerships.
- **Embrace self-compassion:** It's vital to embrace your imperfections and recognize that they are a natural part of being human. Instead of getting caught up in self-criticism or comparing yourself to others, you can choose to accept your flaws and mistakes with kindness and understanding. Doing this is good for your mental and emotional well-being.
- **Set realistic expectations:** Aligning your goals with your values brings a sense of purpose and motivation to your journey. When your goals are in line with what truly matters to you, you are more likely to stay committed and find fulfillment throughout the process.
- **Take good care of yourself:** Did you know that overworking yourself is a form of neglecting self-care? Taking breaks is a key component that promotes physical, mental, and emotional rejuvenation. Creating space for self-care not only replenishes your energy but

also restores your sense of balance and enhances your overall quality of life.

- **Approach trusted adults for advice:** Seeking guidance from wise and trusted individuals can provide you with valuable insights, knowledge, and perspectives. It allows you to tap into the wisdom and experiences of others who may have walked similar paths before you. Such individuals can provide guidance and support that help you to make informed decisions and navigate challenges.

- **Develop a strong sense of self and embrace failure as growth:** Instead of allowing failure to demoralize you, you have the option to approach it with an open and inquisitive mindset. Acknowledging failure as an inherent aspect of the journey of learning is key. By adopting a more positive mindset, you also shift your focus from dwelling on the negative aspects of setbacks to actively seeking the lessons that they offer. Instead of allowing failure to define you, use it as a stepping stone toward progress and personal development.

- **Practice and nurture assertiveness:** Clearly state your thoughts, feelings, and desires without infringing on the rights of others. By expressing your boundaries, you establish limits on what you find acceptable or comfortable in various aspects of your life. It's crucial to remember that assertiveness should be practiced with respect. Respecting others' perspectives, opinions, and feelings is essential for maintaining positive relationships. When you communicate assertively with respect, you treat others with dignity, kindness, and understanding. This helps to foster an environment of open dialogue, empathy, and mutual respect.

- **Manage social media consumption and focus on the present:** Managing social media consumption and focusing on the present are two crucial aspects of maintaining a healthy balance in today's digital age. It's easy to get caught up in the constant stream of information and distractions that social media offers. Direct your attention, energy, and mindset toward the current moment and what is happening right now, as it encourages you to fully engage in the present experience rather than being consumed by thoughts of the past or worries about the future.

The chapter emphasized what truly energizes and motivates you. It highlighted how you can connect with the activities that you love while bringing you fulfillment and a sense of purpose. We emphasized setting SMART goals that are specific, measurable, attainable, relevant, and time-bound. Congratulations on embracing confidence and enthusiasm in leading a balanced and healthy life. Your commitment to personal growth and well-being is truly inspiring! It's amazing to see your limitless potential for success unfold as you navigate life with such positivity and determination. Keep up the fantastic work, and always keep in mind that you possess the ability to accomplish anything you commit your thoughts and determination to. Congrats!

CONCLUSION

During your teenage years, a lot of changes are happening in your physical body. Most of these changes come with hormonal adjustments that also impact your emotional and psychological state. This is why some teenagers are easily irritable, even when they try so hard to be better. The changes that come with puberty can negatively impact your life if they are not properly handled, which is why this book is a great tool on your shelf. You can harness the energy that is associated with your teenage years and direct it toward building a better "you" in preparation for adulthood.

This book introduced you to the B.R.A.V.E.S.T. method of building your mental capacity as a teenager. Here is a quick summary of this framework as presented in this book:

- **B** stands for "believe in yourself and feel good." This aspect of the framework was tackled through chapters 1 and 2. In these chapters, we emphasized the various pillars that improve your self-esteem to a state where you believe in yourself more. These aspects include pampering yourself with self-love and taking good care of your being.

- **R** stands for "resilience and grit." This is where your risk-taking capacity is molded for the better. Chapters 3 to 6 were designed to address your resilience by exploring issues such as how to deal with bullies and substance abuse. You were also enlightened on how you can survive in school-related aspects.

- **A** stands for "accept and adapt to change." As mentioned earlier, teenage years come with many changes, be it physically, emotionally, or otherwise. The nuggets that are provided by the B.R.A.V.E.S.T. framework help you deal with these changes accordingly. Chapters seven and eight tackled this aspect well. Chapter 7 highlighted how you can navigate through various changes, even those that are related to the environment. Chapter 8 focused on the hormonal changes that are associated with the stage that you are in.

- **V** stands for "visualization and positive thinking," which was exclusively addressed in Chapter 9. In this chapter, you were trained to be a "dreamer" whose visualizations come into being.

- **E** stands for "emotional regulation and stress management." There is no doubt that teenage life can come with many emotional issues and stress, both of which need proven techniques to deal with them. Chapters 10 and 11 made it easier for you to get that done by teaching you how you can better control your still-growing brain. You were also provided with tips that you can apply if you find yourself in stressful situations.

- **S** stands for "social matters and empathy." Humans are social beings, and teenagers are not excluded. This is why it is important for you to "find your tribe," as highlighted in Chapter 12. While you are building connections and lasting relationships, you need to be careful not to fall prey to peer pressure. Conflict resolution techniques were also covered. Chapter 13 further explored family settings and your role as a teenager. Considering that a lot of associations are going online, Chapter 14 was prepared to discuss how you can safely navigate social media platforms.

- **T** stands for "tomorrow and times to come," which is a peep into the future. This aspect of the framework was covered by Chapter 15, and it involves setting SMART goals that will help you realize your dreams.

Remember, this is the stage when you are naturally inclined to take risks. Now, did you know that being a risk-taker is one of the strong attributes that business people have? This means you can align yourself to increased chances of making money! Not only that, but risk-taking abilities are also associated with creativity. This is because creativity involves going beyond the status quo. Think of the common social media platform

Facebook. Did you also know that when Mark Zuckerberg launched Facebook in February 2004, he was only 19 years old? In only 10 months, the platform had about a million users who were active. This innovative venture that Zuckerberg pulled in his teenage years has made him the billionaire that he became during his adulthood. Never underestimate your teenage years. Harness the power of mental toughness and embark on a transformative journey toward personal growth, resilience, and lasting success!

REFERENCES

Aldranaris, D. (2023a, July 23). *StoryStar*. https://www.storystar.com/story/ 25589/dreyri-aldranaris/fiction/fairy-tales-fantasy

Aldranaris, D. (2023b, July 30). *StoryStar*. https://www.storystar.com/story/ 25611/dreyri-aldranaris/fiction/drama-human-interest

Ali, Z. (2023, August 11). *StoryStar*. https://www.storystar.com/stories-cate gory/1/true-life

Assistant Secretary for Public Affairs (ASPA. (2019, September 24). *What teens can do*. StopBullying.gov. https://www.stopbullying.gov/resources/teens

Better Health. (n.d.). *Teenagers and sleep*. https://www.betterhealth.vic.gov.au/ health/HealthyLiving/teenagers-and-sleep

Board, K. N. (2021, November 24). *How to adapt to new environments*. Knustnoticeboard. https://knustnoticeboard.info/how-to-adapt-to-new-environments/

Brenner, A. (2015, December 27). *5 benefits of stepping outside your comfort zone*. Psychology Today. https://www.psychologytoday.com/us/blog/in-flux/ 201512/5-benefits-stepping-outside-your-comfort-zone

Capecchi, S. (2022, June 8). *Mindfulness for teens: How it works, benefits, and 11 exercises to try*. Choosing Therapy. https://www.choosingtherapy.com/ mindfulness-for-teens/

Cherry, K. (2022, November 7). *What is emotional intelligence?* Verywell Mind. https://www.verywellmind.com/what-is-emotional-intelligence-2795423

Chinnis, M. (2021, March 29). *The most commonly used drugs by teens*. Principles Academy for Adolescent Wellness. https://adolescentwellnes sacademy.com/the-most-commonly-used-drugs-by-teens/

CNN. (2018, March 15). *20 teen inventions that changed the world*. CNN. https://edition.cnn.com/2018/03/14/world/gallery/20-young-inventors-who-changed-the-world/index.html

Davis, T. (2022, January 3). *How to believe in yourself*. Psychology Today. https://www.psychologytoday.com/za/blog/click-here-happiness/ 202201/how-believe-in-yourself

Delaney, E. (n.d.). *I'm a short afternoon walk and you're putting way too much pressure on me*. McSweeney's Internet Tendency. https://www.mcsweeneys.

net/articles/im-a-short-afternoon-walk-and-youre-putting-way-too-much-pressure-on-me

DeMers, J. (2020, August 12). *13 visualization techniques to help you reach your goals.* Lifehack. https://www.lifehack.org/883519/visualization-techniques

DreamsQuote. (2023, May 8). *Top 55 funny quotes for teens.* https://www.dreamsquote.com/34-funny-quotes-for-teens/

Earley, B. (2021, March 24). *Stuck in a rut? consider making a vision board.* Oprah Daily. https://www.oprahdaily.com/life/a29959841/how-to-make-a-vision-board/

Gasparovic, J. (2022, June 16). *Be yourself: 7 ways to embrace your uniqueness in life.* The Enemy of Average. https://theenemyofaverage.com/embrace-your-uniqueness/

Gillet, R. (2016, May 5). *Larry Page created Google in his sleep — here's why "sleeping on it" can be legitimately productive.* Finance.yahoo.com. https://finance.yahoo.com/news/productive-while-youre-sleeping-125100995.html

Gordon, S. (2014, February 27). *8 reasons why teens bully others.* Verywell Family. https://www.verywellfamily.com/reasons-why-teens-bully-others-460532

Gordon, S. (2017, October 27). *6 types of bullying every parent should know about.* Verywell Family. https://www.verywellfamily.com/types-of-bullying-parents-should-know-about-4153882

Hall, S. H. (2022, December 20). *What does it mean to be authentic?* Business Envato Tuts+. https://business.tutsplus.com/tutorials/what-does-it-mean-to-be-authentic--cms-40517

https://www.facebook.com/familystudies. (2019). *Faith: An overlooked tool in substance abuse prevention and recovery.* Institute for Family Studies. https://ifstudies.org/blog/faith-an-overlooked-tool-in-substance-abuse-prevention-and-recovery

https://www.facebook.com/verywell. (2019). *Steps to teaching your teen how to make good decisions.* Verywell Family. https://www.verywellfamily.com/steps-to-good-decision-making-skills-for-teens-2609104

Hudgins, V. (2021, April 9). *47 funniest teenage quotes and captions.* Darling Quote. https://darlingquote.com/funny-teenage-quotes/

John Muir Health. (2019). *Nutrition for teens.* Johnmuirhealth.com. https://

www.johnmuirhealth.com/health-education/health-wellness/childrens-health/nutrition-teens.html

Johns Hopkins Medicine. (n.d.). *Exercising for better sleep.* Www.hopkinsmedicine.org. https://www.hopkinsmedicine.org/health/wellness-and-prevention/exercising-for-better-sleep

Kehoe, J. (2022, October 5). *How to embrace change: 6 ways to navigate uncertainty.* Mind Power. https://www.learnmindpower.com/embracing-change/

Kids Helpline. (2019, February 23). *Here's how to develop a positive body image.* Kids Helpline. https://kidshelpline.com.au/teens/issues/developing-positive-body-image

Lewis, R. (2021, January 22). *Recognizing the types of bullying and potential effects.* Healthline. https://www.healthline.com/health/childrens-health/types-of-bullying

Lohmann, R. C. (2016, November 22). *10 ways to meet new people: A message for teens.* Psychology Today. https://www.psychologytoday.com/za/blog/teen-angst/201611/10-ways-meet-new-people-message-teens

Lowe, R. C. (2019, January 8). *How to keep a positive attitude as a teenager.* Get off Your Attitude. https://getoffyourattitude.com/how-to-keep-a-positive-attitude-as-a-teenager/

Martin, J. (2017, January 18). *Making a way in the wilderness: embracing change.* LifeTeen.com for Catholic Youth. https://lifeteen.com/making-way-wilderness-embracing-change/

Mayo Clinic . (2023, February 22). *Teen drug abuse: Help your teen avoid drugs.* Mayo Clinic; Mayo Clinic Staff. https://www.mayoclinic.org/healthy-lifestyle/tween-and-teen-health/in-depth/teen-drug-abuse/art-20045921

Menstrupedia. (2019). *Emotional changes that occur during puberty.* Menstrupedia.com. https://www.menstrupedia.com/articles/girls/emotional-changes

McLean Hospital. (2022, January 5). *The mental health impact of bullying on kids and teens.* www.mcleanhospital.org. https://www.mcleanhospital.org/essential/bullying-kids-teens

MILLER, K. (2019, June 19). *You really gotta step out of your comfort zone already: Here's how to actually do it.* Well+Good. https://www.wellandgood.com/stepping-out-of-your-comfort-zone/

Mints, M. (2020, December 14). *How to turn failure into success.* An Idea (by

Ingenious Piece). https://medium.com/an-idea/how-to-turn-failure-into-success-846bea1f4bb0

Monroe, J. (2017, July 14). *Why failure is healthy for...* Newport Academy. https://www.newportacademy.com/resources/empowering-teens/why-failure-is-healthy-for-teens/

Monroe, J. (2018, September 7). *How to cultivate positive teen body...* Newport Academy. https://www.newportacademy.com/resources/well-being/teen-body-image/

Muscle relaxation activity for children, teenagers and parents. (n.d.). Raising Children Network. https://raisingchildren.net.au/guides/activity-guides/wellbeing/muscle-relaxation-activity-children-parents

Nersesian, M. (2021, July 9). *Smells like teens and tweens: How to deal with body odor.* Childrenswi.org. https://childrenswi.org/newshub/stories/teen-body-odor

Newport Academy. (2017, April 5). *Positive thinking for teens.* Newport Academy. https://www.newportacademy.com/resources/mental-health/positivity-teen-mental-health/

Nivedita. (2019, June 28). *Emotional and physical changes during puberty.* Moma Baby Etc. https://momababyetc.com/emotional-and-physical-changes-during-puberty/

Pacheco, D. (2020, December 11). *How a lack of sleep may increase calorie consumption.* Sleep Foundation. https://www.sleepfoundation.org/sleep-deprivation/lack-sleep-may-increase-calorie-consumption

Perry, E. (2022, June 8). *How to believe in yourself and why it matters.* BetterUp.com. https://www.betterup.com/blog/how-to-believe-yourself

Planet Fitness. (n.d.). *10 physical and mental benefits of exercise for teens.* Planet Fitness. https://www.planetfitness.com/community/articles/10-physical-and-mental-benefits-exercise-teens

Planned Parenthood. (2019). *Planned parenthood.* https://www.plannedparenthood.org/learn/teens/puberty

Pontchartrain Pedriatics. (2019, January 14). *5 reasons why teens need to eat healthy.* www.pontchartrainpediatrics.com. https://www.pontchartrainpediatrics.com/5-reasons-why-teens-need-to-eat-healthy

Prasad, A. (2015, November 28). *8 steps for embracing your uniqueness.* Dr. Asha. https://drashaprasad.com/self-awareness/embrace-your-uniqueness/

Puberty: helping your child handle the changes. (2021, April 27). Raising Children

Network. https://raisingchildren.net.au/pre-teens/development/puberty-sexual-development/puberty-helping-your-child

QuoteGram. (2023). *Hilarious teenage quotes about school. QuotesGram.* Quotesgram.com. https://quotesgram.com/hilarious-teenage-quotes-about-school/

Raising Children. (2018, December 13). *Nutrition and healthy food for teenagers.* Raising Children Network. https://raisingchildren.net.au/teens/healthy-lifestyle/daily-food-guides/nutrition-healthy-food-teens

Raising Children Network. (2019, February 5). *Stress in teenagers.* Raising Children Network. https://raisingchildren.net.au/pre-teens/mental-health-physical-health/stress-anxiety-depression/stress-in-teens

Rehab Spot. (2023). *What are the health effects of teen substance abuse?* Rehab Spot. https://www.rehabspot.com/family/health-effects-teen-substance-abuse/

Rosen, A. (2022, September 29). *How dreams become goals and goals become reality.* Forbes. https://www.forbes.com/sites/andrewrosen/2022/09/29/how-dreams-become-goals-and-goals-become-reality/?sh=15a40ac23610

Safefood. (n.d.). *Teenagers.* Safefood. https://www.safefood.net/family-health/teens

Santiago, R. A. (2019, August 29). *20 healthy alternatives to drug use.* AION Recovery. https://aionrecovery.com/articles/20-healthy-alternatives-to-drug-use/

7 ways to combat negative self-talk. (2018, May 4). Drug Rehab & Alcohol Addiction Treatment Centers. https://footprintstorecovery.com/blog/combat-negative-self-talk/

Soul Salt. (2021, July 13). *How to believe in yourself (in 5 simple steps).* https://soulsalt.com/how-to-believe-in-yourself/

Stade, L. (2017, February 5). *The 10 emotional skills every teen needs to be taught.* Linda Stade Education. https://lindastade.com/the-emotional-skills-every-teen-needs-to-be-taught/

Stojšin, T. (2016, December 23). *Adapting to new surroundings: Psychologist tips and stories of three students.* Youth Time Magazine. https://youthtimemag.com/adapting-to-new-surroundings-psychologist-tips-and-stories-of-three-students/

StopBullying.gov. (2019, September 24). *Effects of bullying.* StopBullying.gov. https://www.stopbullying.gov/bullying/effects

Stress and stress management: Pre-teens and teenagers. (n.d.). Raising Children

Network. https://raisingchildren.net.au/pre-teens/mental-health-physi cal-health/stress-anxiety-depression/stress-in-teens

Suni, E. (2020, August 5). *Sleep for teenagers.* Sleep Foundation. https://www. sleepfoundation.org/teens-and-sleep

The scared little mouse, moral stories, short stories, English grammar. (n.d.). English for Students. https://www.english-for-students.com/the-scared-little-mouse.html

13 tips for managing teen acne. (n.d.). Mayo Clinic Health System. https://www. mayoclinichealthsystem.org/hometown-health/speaking-of-health/tips-for-managing-teen-acne

UNICEF. (2023, February). *Cyberbullying: What is it and how to stop it.* UNICEF. https://www.unicef.org/end-violence/how-to-stop-cyberbullying

Water Science School. (2019, May 22). *The water in you: Water and the human body. U.S. Geological Survey.* https://www.usgs.gov/special-topics/water-science-school/science/water-you-water-and-human-body

WebMD Editorial Contributors. (2023, May 16). *How regular exercise benefits teens.* WebMD. https://www.webmd.com/teens/benefits-of-exercise

25933110R00096